OECD Public Governance Reviews

The Irish Government Economic and Evaluation Service

USING EVIDENCE-INFORMED POLICY MAKING
TO IMPROVE PERFORMANCE

This document, as well as any data and map included herein, are without prejudice to the status of or sovereignty over any territory, to the delimitation of international frontiers and boundaries and to the name of any territory, city or area.

Please cite this publication as:
OECD (2020), *The Irish Government Economic and Evaluation Service: Using Evidence-Informed Policy Making to Improve Performance*, OECD Public Governance Reviews, OECD Publishing, Paris, *https://doi.org/10.1787/cdda3cb0-en*.

ISBN 978-92-64-49055-0 (print)
ISBN 978-92-64-66724-2 (pdf)

OECD Public Governance Reviews
ISSN 2219-0406 (print)
ISSN 2219-0414 (online)

Photo credits: Cover © Jenny Donohoe, Department of Public Expenditure and Reform.

Corrigenda to publications may be found on line at: *www.oecd.org/about/publishing/corrigenda.htm*.
© OECD 2020

The use of this work, whether digital or print, is governed by the Terms and Conditions to be found at *http://www.oecd.org/termsandconditions*.

Foreword

Governments are facing growing pressures to deliver public services to citizens and businesses in a complex, fragmented and unpredictable environment. Evidence-informed policy making has a crucial role to play in designing, implementing and delivering better public policies, and thus the potential to improve public sector performance. However, in reality, connecting evidence and policy making remains a constant challenge. Institutional gaps, insufficient skills and capacity, and a lack of an effective knowledge brokering function are common barriers to the use of evidence in policy making. In response to these challenges, many governments are strengthening the 'evidence ecosystem' by investing in strategies to build capacity for policy design and *ex ante* and *ex post* evaluation.

The Irish Government Economic and Evaluation Service (IGEES) is an integrated cross-government service that supports better policy formulation and implementation across the civil service with economic and analytical skills. The purpose of IGEES is to expand the civil service's analytical capacities for evidence-informed policy making. IGEES has strengthened the analytical capacity across ministries and the Irish Civil Service as a whole. IGEES has built a robust evidence base for better policy and decision making.

This OECD study analyses the institutional features and governance of IGEES in light of international best practices, offering an analysis of its processes, tools and people management. The study's recommendations will inform IGEES' Medium-Term Strategy for 2020-23. It was undertaken at the invitation of the Irish Department of Public Expenditure and Reform, which supports the IGEES network, with a view to strengthening evidence-informed policy making in Ireland. At the OECD, this work helps build a comparative understanding of countries' evaluation systems and capacities to promote evidence-informed policy making.

This study is based on the analysis of data collected through qualitative interviews in Ireland with senior civil servants involved in IGEES and related areas of the Department of Expenditure and Reform, current IGEES members based in ministries, and policy officials in ministries. Data was also collected through a questionnaire answered by government departments. Finally, the study draws on examples of existing international practices from OECD work on evidence-informed policymaking and other relevant areas.

This review provides a better understanding of the achievements and remaining challenges for IGEES in putting evidence-informed policy making into action. Linking evidence to ways in which governments can improve performance and better serve their citizens is a fundamental contribution of sound public governance.

Acknowledgements

This report was prepared in the OECD Directorate for Public Governance (GOV) under the leadership of Marcos Bonturi. It is part of the work programme of the Governance Reviews and Partnerships Division, headed by Martin Forst.

The report was drafted by Daniel Acquah, policy analyst at the OECD at the time of drafting, under the strategic direction of Stephane Jacobzone, Head of Unit for evidence, monitoring and policy evaluation. Anne Pauline de Cler contributed some sections and provided highly valuable research assistance. Editorial and production support was provided by Ciara Muller.

The authors are grateful to representatives from Irish government Departments and experts from the Irish Government Economic and Evaluation Service (IGEES) for their valuable contributions and effort to provide all relevant data and mobilise relevant stakeholders. In particular, the OECD would like to thank Jasmina Behan, Daniel O'Callaghan and her colleagues at the Department of Public Expenditure and Reform (DPER) headed by Secretary General Robert Watt. The Secretariat would like to thank the respondents to questionnaires in 12 government departments, and the participants in the interviews that took place in Dublin in May and June 2019. These in-depth interviews were instrumental in further improving the OECD's understanding of the IGEES institutional context and governance. The Secretariat also wish to thank Ms. Francoise Maurel, Director of dissemination and regional action of INSEE (French National Institute of Statistics and Economic Studies) for her participation as a peer reviewer in the process.

The report received detailed and comprehensive feedback from Irish officials. Inside the Secretariat, the authors wish to acknowledge the feedback and contributions received from Jacob Arturo Rivera Perez, Benjamin Welby, Scherie Nicol, Andrew Blazey, and Bagrat Tunyan in the Public Governance Directorate.

Table of contents

Foreword	3
Acknowledgements	5
Executive Summary	9
1 Key findings	**11**
Drivers of change	12
The current OECD study	13
Achievements and Remaining Challenges	13
Recommendations for the future	14
Overall organisation	19
Governance of IGEES	27
References	29
Notes	30
2 Processes, tools and people	**31**
People	32
Tools	36
Processes	38
References	40
Notes	40
3 Overall effectiveness of IGEES and areas for further investment	**41**
Remaining barriers to evidence informed policy making	42
Overall effectiveness and key areas for further investment	46
References	53
Note	55
Annex A. Papers Published by IGEES since 2016	57

Figures

Figure 1.1. Machinery of government involved in EIPM: The horizontal role of IGEES	21
Figure 1.2. IGEES Governance Structures and the interactions between them	27
Figure 2.1. The IGEES Clusters of Skill Needs [pillars of learning]	34
Figure 3.1. Data governance in the public sector	45

Follow OECD Publications on:

 http://twitter.com/OECD_Pubs

 http://www.facebook.com/OECDPublications

 http://www.linkedin.com/groups/OECD-Publications-4645871

http://www.youtube.com/oecdilibrary

 http://www.oecd.org/oecddirect/

Executive Summary

The Irish Government Economic and Evaluation Services (IGEES) supports an integrated approach to policy formulation and implementation in the civil service based on economic and analytical skills. IGEES was created in March 2012 with the aim of expanding analytic capacities for evidence-informed policy making following the budgetary pressures created in the aftermath of the global financial crisis. IGEES's role was to build and extend capacity to achieve value-for-money in policy making across all government departments. The goal is to ensure that a range of public interventions and public expenditure decisions are informed by quality economic analysis and contribute to better outcomes for citizens. This is achieved by placing IGEES staff in all government departments, as well as through specific recruitment, learning and development processes. The IGEES launched a Medium-Term Strategy (MTS) for 2016-2019 to improve the quality of its output, increase the impact of policy analysis process and better inform the policy debate as well as to further develop IGEES as a whole-of-government service.

This OECD study looks at the key institutional features and governance of IGEES in light of international good practices, and offers an analysis of its processes, tools, people management and impact. It identifies current achievements, as well as remaining barriers.

Despite a context of relatively constrained human resources in the Irish Civil Service, IGEES has helped strengthen the overall analytical capacity across departments and built a robust evidence base for better policy and decision making. With resources spread across a large number of Departments, IGEES has helped to deliver a large number of analytical outputs in a variety of policy areas. It has thus contributed to various decision-making processes, such as the development of new regulations and the assessment of programme effectiveness, including through spending reviews. The assessment of spending proposals helps improve the quality and effectiveness of public expenditure.

Despite the progress made, there are several areas where improvement is needed. Data availability and use is one such area, as Ireland does not have an integrated data infrastructure, and access to data across departments remains difficult. There is therefore scope for IGEES to develop a strategy to strengthen evidence and promote "smart" data. Creating leadership for analytical work and its use in government departments is another area requiring attention. Given the robust job market in Ireland, it is important that IGEES branding help attract high-quality candidates in economic and analytical positions.

The study offers four main recommendations to support the development of IGEES within its broader strategic environment and to inform policy development in Ireland in the medium term.

First, greater coherence is needed in the governance of IGEES. The service currently has a broad reach across all government departments, but its governance remains fragmented. For shared ownership of IGEES across government and the country as a whole, OECD recommends that the "Policy Oversight Group" and the "External Advisory Group" form a co-ordinated "Advisory Group" that should function as a "Strategy Board". A corollary would be to rename the internal advisory group as an "Internal IGEES Steering Group", which would better reflect its managerial function. While IGEES has helped create a skills base, it will be important to establish the foundations for a policy on evidence-based policy making to increase access and use of data. This could build on current efforts to promote Open government data, but needs to go well beyond that. IGEES should continue to improve co-ordinate with the statistical office and foster greater access to administrative data. In addition, these efforts should be integrated with broader civil service renewal strategies.

Second, it will be important to further develop peoples' skills and to foster a policy community across the Irish Civil Service. This would entail developing a marketplace and electronic community tools for IGEES analysts, and increasing staff engagement. It will also be important to explore the possibility of developing career opportunities for the analytical professions. IGEES could also continue diversifying its professional expertise, by including other social and applied sciences to strengthen its scope, quality of work and staff motivation. To fully achieve its potential as a cross-cutting service, IGEES should further invest in increasing staff mobility.

Third, it will be important to leverage IGEES to improve the quality and promote greater use of evaluation in Ireland. Complementing IGEES' analytic tools with well-being approaches would both bring the service closer to international good practices in policy analysis and broaden its scope. This could entail reviewing and enhancing the tools and guidelines to broaden their scope. In addition, it would be important to enhance the focus on implementation and theory of change. Finally, IGEES should consider strengthening its capacity for evidence synthesis and knowledge management, using meta-analysis and systematic reviews. These latter are not yet well developed in Ireland's evidence-informed policy-making system. It will also be important to improve mechanisms for using of evidence, sharing best practices and better sharing findings and economic evaluation with Parliament.

Fourth, IGEES should broaden the scope of its dissemination and sharing processes. It needs to continue organising high-level events, branding its analytical work and encouraging its analysts to participate in policy conferences and dialogue. These initiatives could be expanded by connecting with international experts and enlarging the scope of the domestic policy discourse. Establishing mechanisms for peer-to-peer exchanges and sharing work at more junior levels, particularly the more isolated analysts, would help build a broad community of practice. Finally, the branding and dissemination strategy of IGEES could be consolidated by expanding on social media and broaden ownership of the service beyond DPER.

1 Key findings

This chapter presents the key findings from the review, together with an assessment of the achievements and remaining challenges. It underlines the role that IGEES has made to strengthening policy making in Ireland and offers suggestions for achieving greater coherence in the governance of IGEES, for broadening the development of people and skills, for leveraging IGEES to further the quality and use of evaluation in Ireland, and also for furthering the scope of dissemination and sharing processes. The chapter also presents the machinery of government involved in EIPM and discusses the distribution of policy analysis resources across departments as well as their relations with statistical resources and data.

Drivers of change

The Irish Government Economic and Evaluation Service (IGEES) was created in March 2012 under an initiative to extend analytic capacities for evidence-informed policy making across whole of Government in the aftermath of the global financial crisis. The development of the Service sought to expand and extend analytical capacity within the Irish Civil Service.

Previously, there were specific areas of the Irish Civil Service that had dedicated economic and evaluation resources. For instance, resources were present within the Departments of Finance, Transport and Agriculture. Within the Department of Finance, a Central Expenditure and Evaluation Unit (CEEU) had been established in 2006 to promote the application of best value for money practice in public expenditure programmes and projects. Its primary goal consisted in providing analytic and research support to the Department of Finance and later the Department of Public Expenditure and Reform (DPER), while the responsibility for achieving value for money remained in the hands of the relevant Departments and Implementing Agencies. The CEEU assisted these bodies by promoting best practices in the evaluation and implementation of programme and project expenditure and providing guidance now captured in the Public Spending Code. Overall, the CEEU conducted the study of crosscutting issues, complementing the more programme-specific analyses conducted by regular staff in Vote sections in DPER, which are overseeing spending by the Line Departments (Department of Public Expenditure and Reform, 2012[1]). The CEEU itself was established to follow an Evaluation Unit in the Department of Finance (NDP/CSF Evaluation Unit) which was set up in the 1990's to provide technical expertise in the areas of evaluation and appraisal.

The severe economic and fiscal context of the 2008 financial crisis exerted very strong pressures on Ireland's public finances. The Irish economy indeed experienced a significant 14% of GDP contraction from 2007 to 2009, with a deficit going up to 14.2% of GDP in 2009 and gross debt growing from 28.9% to 70% of GDP between 2007 and 2009 (OECD, 2011[2]).

The Irish Government implemented a medium term fiscal consolidation strategy from 2008, consisting in permanent expenditure cuts and revenue enhancement measures. Still, pressures on public finances remained, with an ongoing challenge for the management of public expenditure. This is in line with the general tendency for public spending to rise as a share of national income across countries at the international level in the post-crisis period, which reinforces the need for public spending optimisation (Kennedy and Howlin, 2017[3]).

A number of reforms to public administration and the budgetary and fiscal framework were implemented in response to the financial crisis. The OECD conducted in 2008 a review of the public service reforms occurring in Ireland at that time. The main identified challenge for Ireland going forward was to make different parts of the service work in greater cohesion, with a more integrated approach at the national and local levels (OECD, 2008[4]).

The IGEES was established in 2012 as a more systemic response, which would have the aim to build and expand capacity to achieve value-for-money in policy across all Government Departments by ensuring that the appropriate capacity would be created where it would be needed most at departmental level. This initiative moved the development of economic and evaluation resources beyond individual units in specific Departments towards a more general investment in economic and analytical skills. One of the key goals was in particular to ensure that spending reviews and strategic analysis of public expenditure were informed by high quality economic analysis.

Ireland established a second Public Service Reform Plan for 2014-2016, putting forward IGEES as a service to enhance the analytic capacities of the civil service, undertake evaluations of public expenditure and improve analytic resources for policy formulation (Department of Public Expenditure and Reform, 2014[5]). The OECD's assessment of this second reform plan recognised IGEES as an essential asset in building an integrated cross-Government capacity to support better policy formulation, evaluation and implementation in the civil service, supporting reform and supporting progress on cross-cutting challenges (OECD, 2016[6]). IGEES is currently a key initiative led by the Department of Public Expenditure and Reform to support the "Our Public Service 2020" public sector reforms (Department of Public Expenditure and Reform, 2017[7]).

The purpose of IGEES is to provide a cross-Government service supporting better policy formulation and implementation based on economics, statistics, value-for-money analysis and evaluation. This service particularly aims at improving the design and targeting of the Irish Government's policies and contribute to better outcomes for citizens. (IGEES, 2017[8]). Such purpose is achieved by integrating IGEES staff in each Department, adding their specific analytic and policy skills and expertise across whole of Government. In particular, IGEES assists the Government's decision-making process through specialised recruitment, learning and development of staff in policy analysis from a whole of government perspective. IGEES provides high standards of economic and policy analysis and ensures the application of established best practices in policy evaluation, enabling greater effectiveness of policy and programme interventions. Finally, the Service also facilitates policy dialogue between the civil servants, academia, external specialists and stakeholders across the socio-economic spectrum.

The IGEES launched its Medium Term Strategy (MTS) for 2016-2019 to guide the further development of the service following an initial start-up phase. The focus of this strategy was to improve the quality of its output, increase the impact the policy analysis process and better inform the policy debate. In particular, the work plan for 2018 consisted in continuing the development of IGEES as a whole of Government service, and identified the areas of work that should be undertaken by IGEES staff across individual Departments. It focuses on branded output, dissemination and capacity building through recruitment, mobility and training.

The current OECD study

The current OECD Study undertaken at the invitation of DPER will feed in the development of the next Medium Term Strategy, taking stock of the achievements and effectiveness of the IGEES. This offers a unique opportunity to present an external review of the service's impact in light of international best practices. It will help to gauge IGEES effectiveness, its current achievements and remaining challenges from a cross-country perspective informed by recent international developments. Findings from this review are also founded on consultation exercises (survey questionnaire, interviews) undertaken with a number of Departments themselves.

The goal is to identify areas for further progress and to chart a way forward in the medium to long term, with a view to inform future reform effort and strengthen Ireland's approach to evidence-informed policy making.

Achievements and Remaining Challenges

The IGEES has made a significant difference in strengthening the analytical capacity of the Civil Service in Ireland and progress is being achieved in many areas in terms of building a robust evidence base for better policy and decision-making. While not always directly visible, the impact of IGEES across the civil service is widely recognised, helping to inform the development of spending proposals, to improve the quality and effectiveness of public expenditure and to consolidate the underlying analysis of regulatory impacts for new laws and regulations. With resources embedded across a large number of departments, IGEES has contributed to forming an expert community and a unique capacity to assess, inform and discuss key policy choices, around a significant amount and range of Irish public policies and programmes. For example, IGEES has played a significant role in informing the development of the most recent 28 spending reviews that were released in the autumn of 2019, and is a very active contributor to the Dublin Economics Workshops[1]. The decentralised approach adopted by IGEES, namely having IGEES staff embedded within ministries, has helped to create a cross sectoral networked approach to economic evaluation across ministries.

This has led to significant change across the civil service. Departments have often cooperated to work on analysing key policy issues across the whole of Government. Relevant recent analytical and statistical outputs achieved by IGEES economists and evaluators touch on topics such as health, the environment, disability or Brexit. Table in Annex A presents a more detailed but non-exhaustive overview of the large amount and variety of work that IGEES has achieved across different policy areas between 2016 and 2019, including several Social Impact Assessments. More than 200 papers have been produced by IGEES policy analysts, covering most policy areas such as the Social Protection, Health and Transport, Tourism and Sport [See Annex A].

While papers by themselves are not necessarily a direct proof of policy success, this impressive list testifies of the solid achievements that have been made with limited human and financial resources, within a very compact civil service, compared to some of the larger European or OECD countries.

IGEES is now a recognised brand as part of the policy debate in Ireland and it owes the value of the brand to the commitment, qualification and efforts of all the analysts that are serving IGEES as a community and the Irish civil service as a whole.

While much progress has been made, it is important to continue investing and strengthening IGEES as a shared public good for the civil service in Ireland. The Recommendations offered below by the OECD are meant to offer some suggestions for policy development over the next 3 to 5 years, as a way to capitalise on the current achievements of IGEES and to help close some of the remaining gaps.

Recommendations for the future

The recommendations below are meant to sustain the future development of IGEES, taking into account its broad strategic environment. The recommendations are also framed in light of the broad implications of the international trends in this area.

Achieving greater coherence in the governance of IGEES

The IGEES structures had grown out of its key connection with DPER, one of the core central departments of the Government in Ireland. The governance structures were designed in the initial phase of IGEES, with a view to facilitate its development. Given now the broad reach of IGEES across government departments in Ireland, it will be important to ensure greater coherence and to facilitate collective ownership of IGEES as a key tool of the civil service as a whole in Ireland. For this reason, some of the current fragmentation between a "Policy Oversight Group", an "Internal Advisory Group" and an "External advisory group", do not seem to fit the future needs of IGEES as a horizontal cross cutting service for the government and the country as a whole.

Create an integrated advisory group

The policy oversight group and the external advisory group should be consolidated into one "Advisory group", which should function as a "Strategy board" for IGEES. It should build on the current participation in the policy oversight group, but expanding the participation to some other departments, including in particular the department of the Taoiseach, and also external experts. The external experts could be selected from the Academia, but also the business world, and could include senior international representatives that are interested in developing strategic capacity for policymaking. It should also of course continue to integrate the presence of ESRI, and could include private sector representatives, experts in the area of big data. This could function as a strategic advisory board for IGEES.

One of the corollary of such change, would be to just adapt and rename the internal advisory group, as an "Internal IGEES Steering Group". Such a group performs an essential function to assist in the daily management, coordination and operations of IGEES. Such a group seems to perform its mission in a useful manner, but its name should clearly distinguish it from the other strategic/advisory board.

Establish the foundations for an evidence based policy making policy to increase access and use of data

While IGEES has been very successful in creating a highly skilled economists' workforce inside the Irish civil service, the full implementation of an evidence-based agenda implies leveraging the data that are available for analytical purposes. The fact that IGEES economists are based in the ministries gives them close access to the data held by those ministries, but it is not always enough to guarantee data interoperability and access, and needs to go hand in hand with further progress on an integrated data infrastructure. Evidenced based policymaking also requires integrated strategies to leverage data within the public sector and to facilitate its use for policy making (OECD, *forthcoming*).

This would imply ensuring that any efforts in the use of data for evidenced-based policy making in Ireland are also in line and coherent with broader data policies in the country, including the Public Service Data Strategy 2019-2023[2] (Department of Public Expenditure and Reform, 2018[9]). In addition, Ireland has a very active "Open Government Data" policy and ranks certainly well on this front in comparison with European neighbours or OECD peers. Still, it is clear that many gaps remain in the possibility to obtain linked data sets, and to create "smart data" for analysis. The IGEES efforts are partly coordinated with those of the Irish Statistical Office, but there seems scope for deepening these efforts and giving them a stronger institutional foundation and political leverage.

In countries such as the United States, or even in France concerning firm datasets, the statistical apparatus has more possibilities of interconnection with administrative datasets, so that data can be available for applied economic studies and policy analysis. This report has highlighted a number of remaining challenges for data availability and use that remain to be tackled. A stronger institutionalisation of the evidence, statistical or data function in some of the ministries coupled with an explicit connection with IGEES might help to resolve some of the gaps. In addition, it would be useful to explore the possibility of setting up special mechanisms within the scope of data protection arrangements, to facilitate data linkages without having to release any confidential information outside of the boundaries where these have been collected.

Increase synergies with broader civil service renewal strategies

IGEES is an essential element that support analytical skills in the Irish civil service to strengthen policy formulation and implementation. IGEES also has mechanisms to engage with a wide range of ministries. The ONE civil service strategy aims to foster the management of the civil service as an integrated organisation, with increased scope for flexibility, and responsiveness. It also promotes continuous learning. This presents IGEES with a unique opportunity to brand itself as a cross cutting initiative across the civil service in Ireland. This can help to promote some of the tools that could be developed and are suggested in this report as core ways to facilitate a more unified structure and policy community on these issues across the various streams of the civil service in Ireland.

Broaden the development of people and skills

As there are currently 160 analysts working across a range of ministries, the policy options presented below are aimed at consolidating the current development of IGEES. The goal is to further strengthen its role in nurturing a corporate policy community in Ireland and to adapt its reach and functioning to its increasing responsibilities across the civil service.

Start developing a market place and electronic community tools for IGEES analysts

Given the increased number of IGEES analysts working across ministries, it might be relevant to start creating shared tools for the profession, such as an intranet site, a community of practice, and access to specific tools such as journals, software or analytical resources that could be relevant for IGEES analysts. Online collaborative communication tools (Slack, Teams, etc.) may also be particularly useful for the analysts who tend to be more isolated or working in Ministries that are relatively less equipped.

Creating a functional market place, with openly advertised positions, and even some form of a coordinated rotation might help to create a sense of a shared approach and a level playing field among IGEES analysts.

Other tools that are frequently used in public sector innovation strategies could be mobilised. This could include creating an "Award", of the IGEES paper of the year, and identifying some IGEES agents as "agent of change", who can nurture and promote innovative and forward looking analytical strategies. This could help to emulate best practices and facilitate the diffusion of innovative tools and ideas across the civil service.

Explore the possibility to develop career opportunities for analytical professions

Given the increased scope of IGEES as a horizontal programme, a striking feature is that IGEES positions remain at the level of the policy officer and assistant principal. There is currently no career path estabp0lished as part of the IGEES system. An important element to take into account is that IGEES analysts still tend to have relatively rapid career progressions and to obtain managerial roles relatively quickly.

Still, the issue should be framed as to how to position the analytical and advisory function within the civil service. While it is important for this function to be close to the policy field to remain relevant, yet, if no specific titles or positions are established, there is also a risk for the "evidence-informed policy making agenda" to lack some form of an institutional and political anchor. This is why a number of countries have created functions such as "Chief economist" or Chief evaluators in Ministries, and this is particularly the case now in the US with the implementation of the evidence act. In Ireland, the situation remains mixed: chief economists or their equivalent, tend to exist in some ministries, but the approach seems to remain scattered and fragmented. It is also the case that a number of Senior Civil Servants (Principal Officers, Assistant Secretaries etc.) have an analytical background (e.g. economists, social scientists etc.).

It might be advisable to start thinking first in strategic ways as to how to position and frame the policy advisory function across a range of ministries, at a level that is currently beyond the reach of the current IGEES programme, which would entail framing positions at the principal officer or assistant secretary levels. While framing the policy advisory function, it would also be relevant to start articulating this with exploring the possibility to establish a career path for IGEES analysts, which would not be automatic but would still entail the possibility to obtain a corporate and visible recognition for the most talented elements.

Diversify professional skills to include social and applied sciences

The IGEES was originally created to form a community of professional economist who could support the analytical functions of the civil service in Ireland. In other countries, the types and range of analytical skills that are needed in the civil service may be at times wider than just economics, while still relying on a range of applied social sciences. In the United Kingdom, the analytical professions includes economists, statisticians, operations research and social sciences. While IGEES has already started to slightly diversify its recruitment it will be important to continue this diversification in order to provide the ministries with the range of analytical skills that are needed, as was the case for example in the health area. Another aspect would also be to allow IGEES economists to develop their careers in terms of expertise, completing PhDs for example, and in some cases keeping teaching appointments or possibilities to engage with the academia. This can help to strengthen the reach of IGEES as well as the quality of the work and motivation of the staff.

Reduce remaining barriers to mobility

The IGEES functions as a transversal service across the civil service in Ireland. As such it already provides significant possibilities for mobility, even if a few remaining barriers have been identified within the scope of the report, whether formal or informal. These are not necessarily easy to tackle as they are related to general management practices in the civil service, some pay differentials that exist across ministries and a greater attractiveness of some of the core departments, including DPER, Finance and the department of the Taoiseach. It might be advisable to reward the possibility for young economists to develop some of the IGEES functions in some of the more peripheral areas, by favouring some moves between the periphery and the centre and to explore ways to reduce some of the current pay differentials that may exist across the profession.

Leverage IGEES to further the quality and use of evaluation in Ireland

The IGEES has served to date mainly as a way to invest in skills and capabilities, and some of the core tools that guide policy evaluation in Ireland are closely related to the spending review process, such as the Public Spending code. The experience of New Zealand and some other European countries has underlined the value that a broader perspective on well-being could bring to the development of modern policy analysis for highly developed OECD economies. While Ireland has weathered the impact of the financial crisis and stands among the relatively wealthier European countries, it might make sense to contribute to adapting some of the analytical approaches.

Review and enhance the tools and guidelines to broaden their scope

This could entail reviewing some of the current analytical tools, to broaden their scope and include some of the well-being approaches, including some of the non-monetary aspect of the analysis, the distributional and environmental impacts. This may contribute to enriching the analysis and to maintaining its broader relevance to strengthen the capacity to reach consensus across Ministries across core long-term issues

Enhance the focus on implementation and theory of change

The IGEES has been created as a community of professional economists trained in analytical tools and statistical methods. Yet, one of the often-neglected aspects of policy proposals in government is related to the capacity to create consensus on policy options, to identify pitfalls for implementation and to use a theory of change approach. The recent OECD work on standards of evidence underlines the importance of ensuring the right conditions for implementation. While it is normal for IGEES economists to have a fairly technical and analytical training, it would also be useful as part of the induction and professional experience in the civil service, to address the policy implementation and political economy of reform aspects of policy proposals. This requires developing some of the soft skills and the capacity to listen to weak signals in the policy and political environment.

Strengthen capacity for evidence synthesis and knowledge management

The IGEES has been developed as a compact and effective analytical service within a small country context, where many ministries have to work with relatively limited staffing capacity. The possibility of using "meta-analysis" and systematic reviews also offers an interesting approach that could complement the need to conduct original analytical work for any new policy question. The meta analysis and systematic reviews are part of the "What Works" approach championed by the United Kingdom, and are used by many Nordic countries and in North America. It offers a cost effective alternative to produce analytical research through systematic scans of the international literature.

This report found limited evidence for these methods to be used in the Irish civil service at present, except for the health intervention area where Cochrane approaches and health technology assessment are part of the landscape. Therefore, the IGEES could play a useful role in spearheading such approaches in some of the policy areas, particularly the social policy sector, or issues such as economic clusters and entrepreneurship which are very important to sustain the future of the Irish economic model.

Strengthen mechanisms for use of evidence

The IGEES has served to strengthen civil service capacity to produce evidence and to locate it close to the policy-making functions. Yet, there are still many gaps in the use of evidence, as is the case in the majority of OECD countries. A range of approaches have been identified to strengthen the capacity to promote evidence informed policy making through use of evaluation and evidence by the OECD, including skills for understanding, obtaining, interrogating and assessing evidence, using and applying it, engaging with stakeholders and evaluating. In addition, the OECD has identified some organisational approaches, such as promoting an evidence agenda, or establishing strategic units or positions to strengthen the knowledge brokerage functions. The rationale for IGEES is very close to many of these initiatives and IGEES tools and convening power could be used to promote such mechanisms across departments and facilitate the sharing of best practice across areas of the civil service in Ireland. For example, the Department for children and Youth Affairs has developed an "Evidence into policy programme", that can be an interesting example to support governmental policy priorities through research and knowledge transfer. Sharing these and other initiatives widely across the civil service may help to address this recurring challenge faced in most countries.

Another channel will be to facilitate the sharing of evaluation and economic analytical approaches with Parliament, through the usual dialogue mechanisms that ministries have to engage with Parliamentarians. This could be flagged through IGEES channels while leaving the departments to best identify how to promote and exploit windows of opportunity. Finally, the setting up of some senior positions, such as chief economists, has also been used across a range of countries as a way to help build demand for evidence by promoting individuals with the range of authority, technical and soft skills that are necessary to engage at the political level.

Further the scope of dissemination and sharing processes

The IGEES has been very active to produce and promote analytical substance across the civil service and beyond in Ireland. The proposals below are aimed at supporting such initiatives and complementing them in some areas.

Continue and expand high level events

IGEES is very active in high-level events, branding analytical work, and encouraging IGEES analyst to engage in conferences and policy dialogue. This is excellent, very important and useful.

This can be deepened and continued. For example, high-level visits by international recognised experts, academics could be used to organise "high level policy dialogues", on core and global issues for the domestic audience of analysts and professional economists across the civil service. This may require leveraging some personal contacts from the Irish academic community and could help to broaden the scope of the domestic policy dialogue.

Establish mechanisms for sharing at the more junior levels

While the high-level conferences are certainly useful and important, the report has also highlighted some remaining gaps at the junior level. In some other countries, for example in the US or France, some mechanisms exist to promote sharing of ongoing work, and peer-to-peer exchange for the junior analysts. This would be particularly useful as a way to foster a community approach and for the more isolated analysts to find a community of peers and colleagues to exchange on going work.

Envisage some stronger branding and dissemination strategy

DPER is already active in branding and disseminating IGEES work, while recognising the need to also ensure departmental ownership on the work that is produced in the sectoral areas. Still, a few steps could be envisaged to further consolidate the branding and dissemination strategy. One could simply be to create a colourful IGEES logo, which could be put on the cover or back cover of documents to indicate IGEES contributions. Another one could also be to establish some social media strategy to brand and promote the results. Ensuring that nuggets of information are duly promoted with links to relevant web pages could contribute greatly to increasing the impact, promoting the brand and disseminating the content of IGEES work.

Overall organisation

Machinery of government involved in EIPM

The IGEES is a horizontal network, embedded across Government Departments supported by the Department of Expenditure and Reform (DPER), which is part of the policy making process and which supports the whole of Irish Government in delivering evidence-informed policymaking (EIPM) by guiding policy research, evaluation and appraisal through a variety of processes and frameworks. The diagram below shows the interconnections between IGEES, DPER, the Department of the Taoiseach (Prime Minister's Office) and the Central Statistics Office (CSO). The aim is to deliver value for money in terms of public spending and delivery of public services, IGEES relies on data as a primary building block for good evidence-informed policymaking. The goal of IGEES is to ensure that government departments can make sense of data and use it to feed into policy-making processes. To deliver this goal, IGEES supports capacity for ex-ante and ex-post evaluation and for monitoring cost effectiveness, output and impact on users across departments. As for public intervention, the areas considered are current expenditure capital expenditure, taxation measures and regulation. In terms of stage of analysis, different requirements are established for the appraisal stage, the implementation or monitoring phase and the evaluation phase.

The Central Statistical Office is a statutory body responsible for the development and analysis of statistics, supports capacity for statistical analysis across a number of departments and agencies with a set of statisticians, who are in some instances associated with IGEES staff across Ministries to help manage data. However, the governance of this statistical network is less developed than in the case of IGEES. While the two are working closely together, there are also no explicit governance arrangements to connect the two.

The Department of Public Expenditure and Reform (DPER) is an integral part of the overall organisation and coordination of policy analysis in Ireland, together with the Department of the Taoiseach and the Ministry of Finance (see Figure 1.1). DPER hosts critical IGEES resources, with the IGEES coordination Unit, with an Accounting Officer, a significant number of IGEES staff located within DPER, and particularly the Vote Sections[3] as they are termed in DPER, which oversee different parts of the budget.

IGEES Staff are located in the main policy units in charge of overseeing expenditure, for example the Health Vote, the Social Protection Vote and the Pay and Pensions Division. In cases where a unit does not have its own IGEES resources, the central IGEES unit in DPER is available to provide support on a project basis. IGEES staff in the Vote Sections within DPER have a critical and ongoing relationship with Departmental policy units and Departmental IGEES staff. DPER's role as a Treasury Department necessitates ongoing engagement with line Departments as part of the budgetary process and expenditure management. As such, IGEES staff would be involved in this on an on-going basis. In addition, IGEES policy analysts would typically engage with the relevant Departments in relation to papers proposed for publication as part of the Quality Assurance process.

The relations between the "Votes" and the departments are by nature challenging at times, between sectoral spending departments and a central expenditure oversight body. The goal of the system is to ensure that final decisions are properly informed by thorough analysis of the facts that can be done through in depth analysis at departmental level and a challenge function operated by DPER. These relations appear to be more fruitful in some sectors than others. The role of DPER has also evolved over time, as the need for fiscal restraint has been felt as less stringent following the economic recovery, which may reduce the impact a pure value for money and expenditure focused approach. This also depends on the quality and availability of dedicated analytical resources within the departments, which remain uneven. In some departments, such as Business Enterprise and Innovation these resources are well developed with a corporate culture that is close to that of DPER facilitating a fluid relationship. In other departments where similar resources also exist, such as health, the policy angle deviates from a pure value for money approach, which makes a dialogue on a common ground more difficult to achieve.

Figure 1.1. Machinery of government involved in EIPM: The horizontal role of IGEES

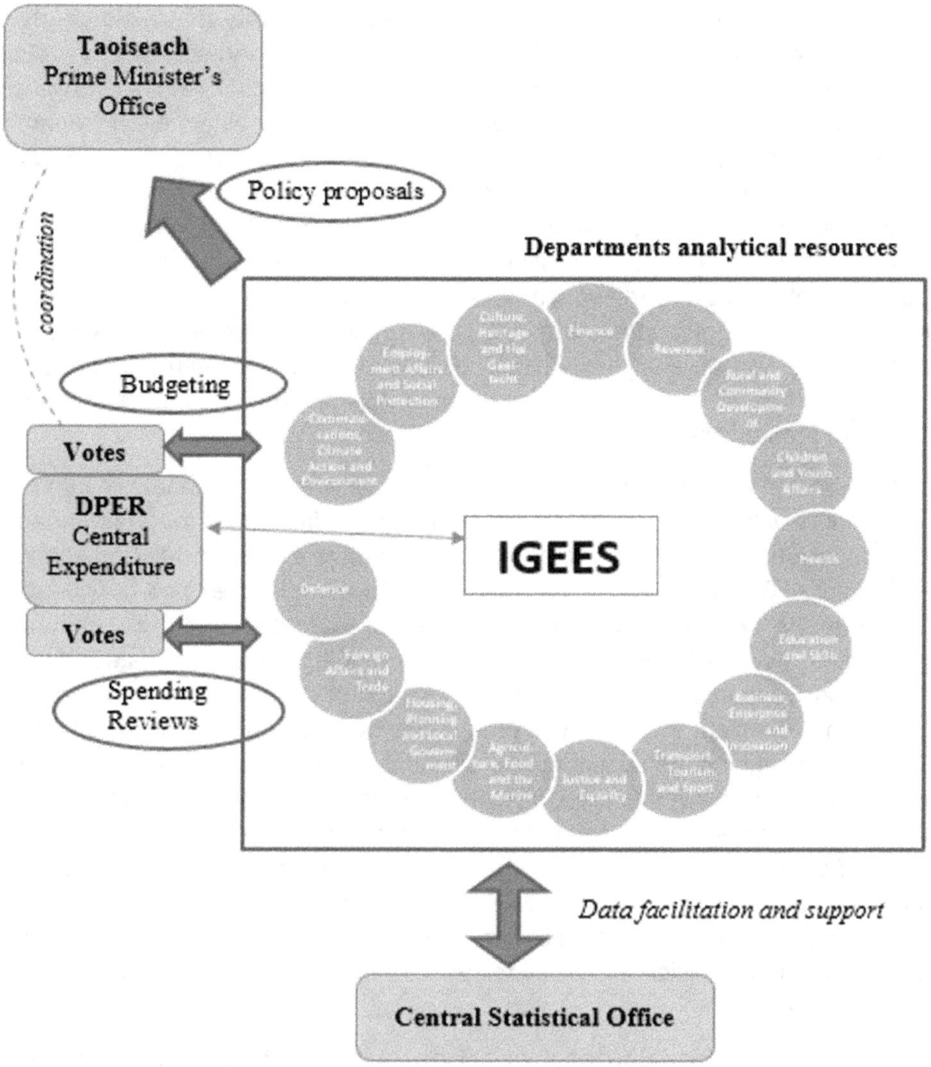

Source: OECD Secretariat, drawing on IGEES related materials and interviews.
Notes: This figure is a schematic presentation, which helps to show some core processes, but in which the role of the agencies could not be shown in full. IGEES resources are present in all of the department analytical resources, as well as in DPER and in Taoiseach.

Policy analysis within DPER and its connections with the Departments

Structure of analytical resources within departments

Departments varied in terms of how they deployed and structured their analytical resource. In some Departments, the policy analysis functions are within given policy units. Some Departments have a unit or units specifically dedicated to economic analysis, which may group IGEES and statistical staff who work on the policy areas their Departments are responsible for. In other Departments, the analysis functions were located in a central unit that also had responsibility for other cross cutting functions such as reform and strategy, alongside policy analysis. These models are not mutually exclusive in the Irish system with some Departments having analysts embedded within policy teams whilst also having one or more specialist units. IGEES typically employs staff at Administrative Officer and Assistant Principal levels, which are key analytic roles in the civil service below senior and managerial grades. [See Box 1.1 for more details on the grade structure of the Irish Civil Service].

There was a trend for Departments with more developed analysis capacity to have organised this into a unit or units specifically dedicated to analysis. In Departments at an earlier stage of developing their analytical capacity, the IGEES staff are typically either located within policy units or in a central cross cutting unit. While attempts to build a critical mass of analytical capacity within each Department appear desirable, a one-size fits all approach may not work best to organise how that capacity should be structured and organised. Each model has its own profile of strengths and weaknesses and context will determine the appropriateness of each model or combination of models for each Department. Analysts embedded within policy units have the advantage of proximity to the policy-making processes, increasing the likelihood of producing timely and policy relevant analysis. The downside is that protecting time for analysis can be difficult in the face of competing pressures and where individual Administrative Officer analysts are not managed by colleagues with an analytical background. In Departments with a unit or units dedicated to policy analysis, it is perhaps easier to provide the critical mass that makes protecting time dedicated to analysis and gives junior staff clearer progression opportunities.

The departments also differ in relation to their ability to incorporate economic analysis into policy thinking which is not always in line with the size of their economic expenditure or economic impact. Again, the Department of Finance, of Business, Enterprise and Innovation have a more developed economic analysis function. The Department of Social Protection has also a relatively well-developed unit, headed by a chief economist recruited from the Central Bank. The Department of Education and Skills has three members of staff that are designated as IGEES resources. The Department also has a dedicated Statistics Unit, the Inspectorate's Evaluation Support and Research Unit, which supports the quality assurance role of the Inspectorate and feeds back into curriculum development. Still overall, there is limited capacity for strategic economic and policy analysis given the size of the department, particularly as a share of total government expenditure. It is worth nothing that in this area, as is the case in several other OECD countries, analytical capacity has been built at arms' length from the department, with the Education Research Centre, established in 1966 and designed as a statutory body in 2015. This Centre conducts independent research as well as evaluations commissioned by the Department of Education and Skills, and provides an assessment support service to educational facilities. Other bodies, include the National Council for Curriculum and Assessment, the National Council for Special Education, the Higher Education Authority, and SOLAS.

Most departments, such as Health and Education and Skills, are also subject to intense political and social pressures where the need for thorough analysis is competing with other political demands. It appears that the department of Health was currently building significant analytical capacity in house, taking into account the role of other disciplines, which are important in the health area, such as social sciences or epidemiology. However, the focused scope of the current study did not allow for a full dialogue and review of all the departments.

> **Box 1.1. Irish Civil Service Grade Structure**
>
> The IGEES stream recruits policy analysts at **Administrative Officer**, and **Assistant Principal**, which are key to the analytic capacity of the service. These are located below higher managerial levels, namely **Principal Officer** (senior management), **Assistant Secretary** and **Secretary General** (highest management grades). The general Civil Service grading structure starts with the **Clerical Officer** grade, reporting to junior management at the **Executive Offer grade, which reports to mid-management grade** Higher Executive Officer. Administrative Officer grade is a graduate entry position and is at the same grade level as the HEO.
>
> Source: Publicjobs.ie « Range of opportunities and roles" https://www.publicjobs.ie/en/information-hub/the-civil-and-public-service/career-path-in-the-public-service, Accessed 10 September 2019.

Statistical resources and data

The Central Statistical Office (CSO), the national statistics body, is another key part of the analytical landscape in Ireland. The remit of the CSO is to collect, analyse and make available statistics about Ireland's people, society and economy. As well as producing official statistics to contribute to evidence informed policy making at a national level across a range of policy areas, at the European level the CSO is also responsible for providing an accurate picture of Ireland's economic and social performance to enable comparisons with other jurisdictions.

In order to strengthen the statistical capacity across the government, the CSO created the Irish Government Statistical Service (IGSS), which involves placing statisticians on secondment in government departments, building on existing secondment models within the Irish civil service. A key part of programme of work for the ISS is contributing towards the development of the National Data Infrastructure (NDI), which aims to improve how the government collects, manages, shares and stores data in order to make it more useful for policymaking.

There are no overall formal explicit coordination arrangements between IGEES and the IGSS, even if they have a number of joint initiatives that aim to create a stronger 'critical mass' of analytical resource in each Department. However, the extent to which IGSS and IGESS staff are integrated and collaborate varies considerably across departments. Where this integration works well, it had the double benefit of leading to improved analysis and improved data quality

The National Data Infrastructure is a work in progress. A number of data linking initiatives have already been progressed across areas including housing[4], incomes[5] and educational outcomes[6]. In fact, while the presence of IGEES and statistical staff at departmental level allows for full exploitation of the departments' statistical resources, significant challenges remain in accessing data across departments, and in obtaining linked files, where coverage of common identifiers to merge datasets is low. A common identifier does not exist yet and is still currently under development for businesses and for citizens, as strong protective legislation restricts access to individual data and does not allow for merging statistical files. Accredited research organisations and researchers can apply to gain access to CSO Research Microdata Files (RMF) through the secure Researcher Data Portal. However, the experience reported by academics to access public data seemed to reflect significant constraints, unless there was a close partnership with a given ministry. The experience from countries such as New Zealand, Denmark and France may nevertheless offer useful insights for the Irish context (Box 1.2)

Ireland recently showed significant progress regarding open government data, as the country ranked first in the European assessment on Open Data maturity for the second year in a row (Open Data Unit (DPER),

2018[10]). Available international results for 2019 tend to show similar progress, with the country catching up to highest performing countries such as Korea, as shown in the results of the OECD Open Useful Reusable data (OURdata) Index[7].

DPER is responsible for the country's Public Service Data Strategy 2019-2023, the open data policy and the Open Data Strategy for 2017-2022 aiming at increasing the value of public sector data for value co-creation (OECD, 2018[11]), through the accessibility to government data in an open and freely reusable way (Department of Public Expenditure and Reform, 2019[12]). The national Open Data Portal provides access to a significant number of datasets, supported for example by the launch of an Open Data engagement fund in July 2019. While these initiatives are highly laudable, and despite these achievements, the use of data for policy purposes and its impacts are still hampered by the absence of a capacity to create linked datasets. The challenge is to create smart datasets, including a range of either firm or individual characteristics that provide the flexibility and resources to perform high-powered analysis, and where IGEES analysts working on the ground in ministries are still facing significant barriers. Countries such as Denmark or New Zealand provide interesting best practice examples of data integration, as national registries in Denmark, and an integrated Data Infrastructure in New Zealand facilitate agile and dynamic analysis and modelling (See Box 1.2).

> **Box 1.2. International experiences in creating national data infrastructures.**
>
> **New Zealand's Integrated Data Infrastructure**
>
> New Zealand's Integrated Data Infrastructure (IDI) represents an innovative approach to administrative data. This large research database links together anonymised administrative data about people, businesses and households and various life events such as education, income, benefits, migration justice and health. The data is provided by government agencies, NGOs and Stats NZ (New Zealand's official data agency) and is accessible by accredited researchers to conduct evaluations. In fact, the IDI is a strong asset that enables quality evaluations to be carried out both within New Zealand's Ministry of Social Development and increasingly by external parties such as academics.
>
> **The Danish system for access to micro data**
>
> Statistics Denmark facilitates register-based research by giving researchers access to anonymised data directly on their own computers. This represents a unique opportunity for researchers to use micro data in their policy work. In Denmark as in other Nordic countries, Personal Identification Numbers (CPR) are used as identification keys in people and business registers, which contribute to a substantial proportion of the national production of statistics. In the Danish register, data from 250 subject areas (such as demography, labour market, consumption, agriculture, housing, transport, environment, trade, etc.) are available for research purposes. Such micro data is accessible to approved public researchers, analysts (from universities, sector research institutes, ministries, etc.), and non-profit and private research organisations. The data is prepared by the Research Service Division and is accessible remotely and securely through specific powerful internet servers. All aggregated results from researchers' computers are stored in special files and printouts are sent to them directly by email, in a continuous process that takes place every 5 minutes. This process is effective and advantageous since all emails are logged at Statistics Denmark and regularly checked by the Research Service Unit. Lastly, the newest versions of several computer packages such as SAS, SPSS, STATA, GAUSS and R are available on the research server.

> **France's Secure Access Data Centre (CASD)**
>
> In France, the statistics system also facilitates research by giving researchers access to anonymised data through a secure access data centre (CASD). The CASD is a trusted interface between data producers and users, enabling secure data depositing and matching. It has become a reference in the provision of secure and remote access to statistical and administrative microdata. For instance, this centre makes publicly available data from the national statistics institute (INSEE), as well as from the Justice, Education, Agriculture and Finance ministries. The CASD also provides external access to private companies' data for collaboration with researchers, start-ups and consultants. Today, it has secured about 350 data sources and shared more than 200 publications.
>
> Sources: Statistics Denmark (2014) *Data for Research* https://www.dst.dk/en/TilSalg/Forskningsservice#. OECD (2019) *The Role of Evidence Informed Policy Making in Delivering on Performance: Social Investment in New Zealand.* CASD website https://www.casd.eu/en/, Accessed 17 October 2019.

Role of IGEES in building analytical capacities across ministries

More than 160 IGEES policy analysts work across all of the Irish Government's Departments, through the general scales and contracts of the civil service, at Assistant Principal (middle management) and Administrative Officer (graduate entry). They are either serving civil servants or staff directly recruited through the open competition process of the IGEES stream. The latter are graduates, experienced economists, evaluators and policy analysts who join analytical resources in all Departments. IGEES posts are funded by host Departments, as direct Departmental placements. Departments validate posts for Administrative Officers (AO) or Assistant Principals (AP) at internal level, and then request that IGEES place them on a list for the next recruitment cohort. The Department that has the most IGEES staff is the Public Expenditure and Reform, which through the IGEES recruitment stream added 11 APs and 22 AOs to an existing cohort of Department's policy analysts. In contrast, IGEES staff is scarcer in all other Departments, ranging from one to five APs or AOs, with the exception of the Department of Finance, which enhanced its existing analytical capacity through the IGEES stream by adding 7 APs and 11 AOs.

IGEES supports capacity building and skills enhancement and transfer for individuals and Departments through relatively more flexible opportunities for mobility, a learning and development framework and targeted opportunities, and platforms for discussion on analytical output and its relevance for policy. The Department of Public Expenditure and Reform has overall policy responsibility for the IGEES and thereby reports on cross-departmental issues such as resourcing, capacity building and continuing professional development under the work programme. The IGEES Research Fund, issued twice in 2018, is another means to support analytical work on cross-departmental issue to break policy silos, particularly the work carried by the Departments of Finance, Children and Youth Affairs and Housing, Planning and Local Government. It also supports the new project undertaken by the Department of Employment Affairs and Social Protection and the Central Statistics Office.

There is almost universal recognition that IGEES was providing a critical role in building capacity across the government and having an analytical 'brand' for economic analysis in this regard was useful and important. Branding and development of IGEES has to build on the fact that there is a need to adopt a comprehensive perspective, with analytical positions that pre-date the existence of the IGEES recruitment stream and many people working in non-IGEES roles but with strong analytical backgrounds, sometimes relying on a wealth of social sciences. Ireland is facing the constraints of the scale of a small country, yet is deploying an astute response to address the challenge even if it is more difficult to foster a multidisciplinary approach. Larger countries such as the UK may have the possibility to develop a broader range of analytical expertise within the civil service: for example, the policy professions in the UK include the economists, the statisticians, the operations research and social scientists.

Distributed analytical functions across the government

While the IGEES is an essential service in building analytical capacity across the Irish Government, it works as part of a policy environment composed of other relevant bodies also contributing to evidence-informed policy making.

In terms of performance audits and ex post evaluation, the Supreme Audit Institution, the Irish Office of the Comptroller and Auditor General plays a key role in improving the use of public resources, optimising public spending and strengthening the accountability of public officials. Many government Departments themselves also have dedicated, and separate, internal audit functions.

The work of the Irish Central Bank is closely interrelated to that of the IGEES, and interestingly, the service and the Central Bank joined efforts in supporting awards for young economists to do research on priority topics, such as the impact of Brexit on the Irish economy (Central Bank of Ireland, 2019[13]). Other institutions support the whole Irish Government in making better policy decisions and sustaining its budget: the Irish Fiscal Advisory Council (IFAC) for instance, is an independent statutory body that was established as part of the agenda to reform Ireland's budgetary architecture. The IFAC has a mandate to assess government revenue and spending as well as macroeconomic and budgetary forecasts (Irish Fiscal Advisory Council, 2019[14]).

Moreover, the National Economic and Social Council supports the Taoiseach and Government by giving guidance on important policy issues with a particular focus on sustainable economic development. Many actors from academia such as the Economic and Social Research Institute (ESRI) and the Irish Economic Association support analytic capacity building in Ireland for the improvement of policymaking. The ESRI for instance plays a significant role in producing high quality independent research to inform policy, support the economy and promote social progress (Economic and Social Research Institute, 2019[15]). The institute has joint research programmes with a number of government departments such as Finance and Housing. Interestingly, it also developed a useful microsimulation model, SWITCH, to assess the impact of tax and pensions as well as a suite of structural macroeconomic models. Lastly, in terms of events, the Annual Irish Economic Policy Conference, part of the Dublin Economics Workshop, also favours the inclusion of economic analysis and evaluation in policy-making.

One of the major institutions with a strong interest in policy analysis is the Parliamentary Budget Office (PBO). The PBO in Ireland has a remit to provide independent and impartial information, analysis and advice to the Houses of the Oireachtas. The PBO is an important source of financial and budgetary information for Oireachtas Members as it conducts ex-ante scrutiny of all budgetary matters. The PBO covers a necessarily broad range of issues: from giving information on the latest changes in legislation and how it will affect the public finances to the costing of policy proposals. As a result, the PBO has produced a number of publications that aim to make IGEES outputs digestible for parliamentarians, and the Oireachtas Library and Research service is also a key resource.

It might be worth exploring whether there could be a stronger connection between the Houses of the Oireachtas and the work of IGEES staffs. There still seemed to be some distance to go to move from most parliamentarians seeing IGEES as an exclusively DPER initiative, to one that is truly shared and owned across government. Whilst recognising that DPER analysis needed to retain a degree of technical autonomy and that there are established structures for Government Departments to engage with the Oireachtas, it could be desirable to make IGEES work more visible at the political level and to increase its broader impact. IGEES staff are part of each Government Department and report to the relevant Secretary General. Ultimately, however, it also remains in the hands of Departments themselves to reach out to Parliament and engage with the issues suggested.

Governance of IGEES

IGEES governance structure and interactions

The governance structure of IGEES consists of several elements, including an Accounting Officer, a Policy Oversight Group, an External Advisory Group and an Internal Advisory Group, as can be visualised in Figure 1.2.

Figure 1.2. IGEES Governance Structures and the interactions between them

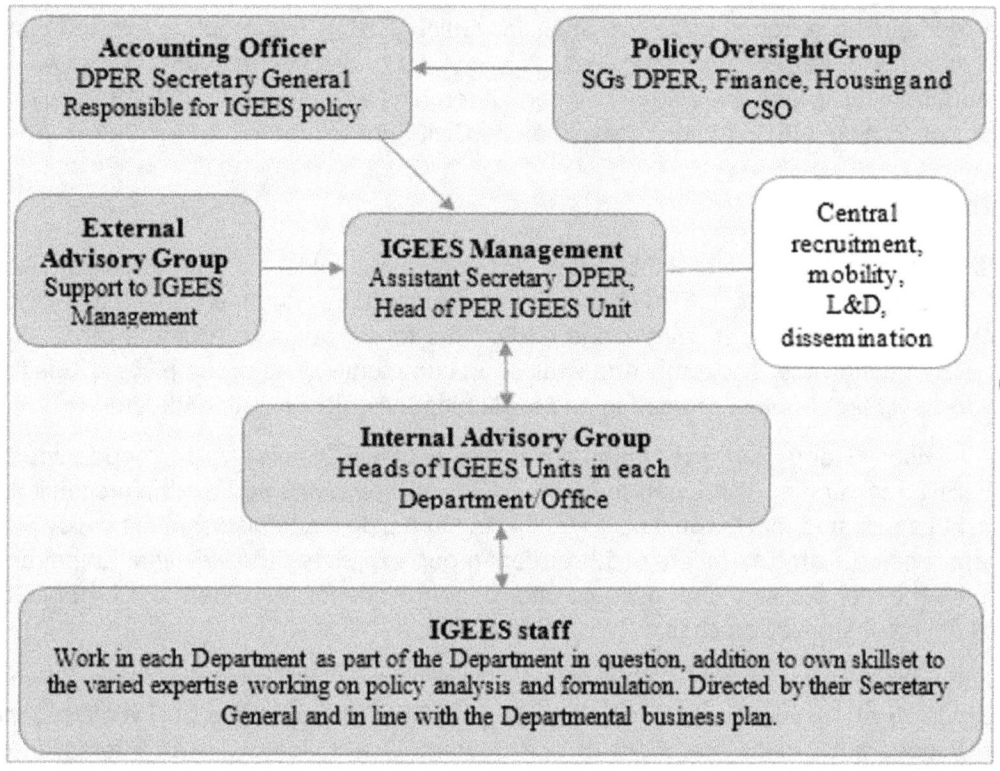

Source: IGEES (2019) OECD Review of IGEES – Overview and Briefing.

Accounting Officer for IGEES

The Secretary General of the Department of Public Expenditure and Reform has overall responsibility for IGEES and is Chair of the Policy Oversight Group. Within DPER, the Head of IGEES has responsibility to implement the IGEES strategy and all its actions. The Head of IGEES reports to an Assistant Secretary in DPER, to the Policy Oversight Group and to the Secretary General DPER. IGEES is also supported by the Internal Advisory Group and the External Advisory Group.

Internal Advisory Group

The internal advisory group performs an important function for the management of IGEES and the daily coordination of IGEES resources. All Departments are represented by a PO on the IGEES Internal Advisory Group, which is chaired by the Head of the IGEES unit in DPER. A cross-departmental forum works towards the development of IGEES throughout the whole government. It drives the implementation of the IGEES strategy at Departmental level. This includes analytical capacity building through recruitment, mobility and Learning and Development, production of analytical outputs and their dissemination through publication, events and awareness raising and championing the culture of evidence informed policymaking. It also reinforces the development and implementation of the IGEES Learning and Development programme.

It seems to benefit from active engagement from the departments involved, which value the contribution of IGEES to their work and see it as a useful forum for exchange, and coordination on staffing issues.

Policy Oversight Group

The Policy Oversight group is composed of the Secretaries General from the Department of Public Expenditure and Reform (DPER), the Department of Finance, one other Department elected on a rolling basis, and a representative from the Central Statistics Office (CSO). The group is a forum that considers the strategic direction of IGEES and meets every six months to discuss relevant issues. As IGEES has grown, the input from this group has also developed. It remains a challenge for IGEES to build on the role of this group to champion IGEES at senior levels of the Civil Service.

External Advisory Group

The External Advisory Group is composed of external stakeholders from research institutes and Universities. It provides support to IGEES management in order to develop the Service by providing advice on important issues such as peer review and CPD. This forum helps to promote the communication between IGEES and the wider economic and evaluation community. The group plays a significant role in the IGEES internship programme, promoting and facilitating the selection of candidates.

The External Advisory Group is engaged in the development of IGEES, playing an important role in helping to promote IGEES recruitment. The External Advisory Group itself welcomed the interaction it had with the IGEES team, but suggested that it would be beneficial to have a dialogue also with the policy professionals within the Departments. Some members of this current group expressed the view that further opportunities to meet with the Internal Advisory Group would offer opportunities for the External Advisory Group to get a greater insight into the policy process.

While it includes the Director of the ESRI, most of its members have limited experience of government, and a limited vision of the implications and the role of IGEES for improving policy effectiveness within government. It does not include members of other external institutions with an interest in developing Evidence Informed Policy Making (EIPM) on a broad basis in Ireland.

Assessment of the effectiveness of current institutionalisation arrangements

There is general recognition, at official level, in Ireland of the contribution that IGEES has made to improving capacity for policymaking and policy effectiveness at the national level. IGEES benefits from a strong institutional setting with its anchor within DPER, although this can be both an asset and a curse as it may also limit its impact if it is perceived as solely working for DPER. IGEES has created an undisputed reputation for professional quality and for improving the standards of economic analysis within government in Ireland, yet the challenges are to ensure that such an innovative institutional framework can be effective from a whole of government perspective.

On a day-to-day basis, the internal advisory group is very effective in driving day to day operations and providing a platform for sharing and coordination. The Policy Oversight Group is comprised of senior management of the Civil Service with the potential to champion the work of IGEES with all senior management. The External Advisory Group has the benefit of consisting of members of academia and Research Institutions who can ensure the development of skilled graduates and knowledge transfers to IGEES. The combination of these groups could lead to a more structured and sustained attention to data and evidence without which IGEES cannot be fully effective.

References

Central Bank of Ireland (2019), *Young economists could win placement at Central Bank of Ireland*, https://www.centralbank.ie/news/article/young-economists-could-win-placement-at-central-bank-of-ireland (accessed on 12 August 2019). [13]

Department of Public Expenditure and Reform (2019), *Gov.ie - Open Data in Ireland*, https://www.gov.ie/en/policy-information/8587b0-open-data/ (accessed on 11 September 2019). [12]

Department of Public Expenditure and Reform (2018), *Public Service Data Strategy 2019-2023*, https://www.gov.ie/en/publication/1d6bc7-public-service-data-strategy-2019-2023/ (accessed on 18 October 2019). [9]

Department of Public Expenditure and Reform (2017), "Our Public Service 2020", https://ops2020.gov.ie/resources/Our-Public-Service-2020-WEB.pdf (accessed on 10 September 2019). [7]

Department of Public Expenditure and Reform (2014), "Public Service Reform Plan 2014-2016", https://reformplan.per.gov.ie/2014/downloads/files/Reform%20Plan%202014.pdf (accessed on 10 September 2019). [5]

Department of Public Expenditure and Reform (2012), *About Us : The Central Expenditure Evaluation Unit | The Public Spending Code*, https://publicspendingcode.per.gov.ie/about-us/ (accessed on 23 July 2019). [1]

Economic and Social Research Institute (2019), *About the ESRI | ESRI*, https://www.esri.ie/about (accessed on 11 September 2019). [15]

IGEES (2017), *IGEES Work Programme for 2018 and IGEES Achievements in 2017*, http://igees.gov.ie/ (accessed on 12 August 2019). [8]

Irish Fiscal Advisory Council (2019), *Irish Fiscal Advisory Council*, https://www.fiscalcouncil.ie/ (accessed on 11 September 2019). [14]

Kennedy, F. and J. Howlin (2017), "Spending reviews in Ireland-Learning from experience", *OECD Journal on Budgeting*, Vol. 2016/2, pp. 93-109, https://www.oecd-ilibrary.org/docserver/budget-16-5jg30cchf0g0.pdf?expires=1565605875&id=id&accname=ocid84004878&checksum=53F7E58BBFC1BEF3E24DE76EFFB045D9 (accessed on 12 August 2019). [3]

OECD (2018), *Open Government Data Report: Enhancing Policy Maturity for Sustainable Impact*, OECD Digital Government Studies, OECD Publishing, Paris, https://dx.doi.org/10.1787/9789264305847-en. [11]

OECD (2016), "Assessment of Ireland's Second Public Sector Reform Plan 2014-2016", https://www.oecd.org/gov/ireland-public-sector-reform-plan-assessment.pdf (accessed on 10 September 2019). [6]

OECD (2011), *Restoring Public Finances*, https://www.oecd.org/governance/budgeting/47558957.pdf (accessed on 2 August 2019). [2]

OECD (2008), "Ireland, Towards an Integrated Public Service", https://www.oecd-ilibrary.org/docserver/9789264043268-en.pdf?expires=1568115320&id=id&accname=ocid84004878&checksum=22A4C83734AC673029BF03301D6EF162 (accessed on 10 September 2019). [4]

Open Data Unit (DPER) (2018), *Ireland achieves first place in its Open Data Maturity assessment for the second year running - data.gov.ie*, https://data.gov.ie/blog/ireland-achieves-first-place-in-its-open-data-maturity-assessment-for-the-second-year-running (accessed on 11 September 2019). [10]

Notes

[1] https://www.dublineconomics.com/.

[2] https://www.gov.ie/en/publication/1d6bc7-public-service-data-strategy-2019-2023/.

[3] A vote section is a subunit of DPER in charge of reviewing budgets and expenditure for certain areas of government.

[4] https://www.cso.ie/en/releasesandpublications/ep/p-rppi/residentialpropertypriceindexjune2019/.

[5] https://www.cso.ie/en/releasesandpublications/ep/pgpii/geographicalprofilesofincomeinireland2016/.

[6] https://www.cso.ie/en/releasesandpublications/ep/p-heo/highereducationoutcomes-graduationyears2010-2016/.

[7] OECD *Government at a Glance 2019*.

2 Processes, tools and people

This chapter analyses the processes that support evidence informed policy making in Ireland and the contribution of IGEES resources, including people to these processes. The chapter addresses recruitment and progression as well as learning and development. It also discusses the tools that are supporting EIPM, including the role of frameworks and guidelines and highlights the need for broadening the analytical framework beyond the spending code. It also underlines the role of the departments' programme of work, and discusses the balance of work conducted internally versus externally.

This section will analyse the processes that support Evidence Informed Policy Making Ireland and the contribution of IGEES to these processes, as well as the tools that are used to support EIPM and the core IGEES that contribution makes through investing in people.

People

Recruitment and progression

One of the main functions of the IGEES unit in DPER is to coordinate the recruitment process for IGEES so that graduates and experienced economists/evaluators/policy analysts can join analytical resources in Departments. As IGEES is an established brand in Ireland among economics graduates, this has ensured a continuous inflow of quality trained professional staff in economics across government. The recruitment process involves on average 20 graduates per year, with an increase in intake in recent years, for a total number of 160 IGEES staff working across the departments. This is for the AO level, in addition, an open competition is organised for APs, with 18 positions filled in 2018. The successful candidates are comprised of a mix of existing IGEES policy analysts, who are being promoted, and policy analysts recruited externally. In addition, in 2018 IGEES introduced a pilot 3-month internship programme. Following on success of the pilot, the internship programme was rolled out in 2019, with the placement of thirteen interns across nine Departments.

Changes to the recruitment processes have been positive, as they have helped to broaden the expertise of the new recruits. IGEES is now recruiting social scientists as well as economists and despite a tightening labour marked, IGEES continues to attract skilled workers.

Opening up the recruitment to social scientists and others increased the diversity of the skill set of the new recruits. One senior manager noted that bringing a diversity of perspectives on a particular policy issues led to higher quality policy analysis. The Public Appointments Service oversees the recruitment processes for IGEES. A panel of qualified candidates results from the competitions and all those who are successful have the necessary skills for the position of IGEES AOs or APs but from time to time Departments may express a desire for more targeted skills. For example, getting health economists through IGEES recruitment processes is challenging, given the competition with the private sector with the pharmaceutical industry. This is also due to the way that current general IGEES recruitment processes are structured, and the fact that there is no guarantee that as a result of these processes, a specialised economist would work in their field. Another example is the Better Regulation Unit in DBEI, which requires more qualitative than quantitative expertise, and where there is a concern to assign jobs that correspond to people's expertise and interests. In some countries such as France, the pool is managed centrally, with a common market place, which provides an opportunity to identify opportunities and facilitate lateral moves, with some central steering.

IGEES had also made further positive changes to the model of recruitment. Originally, IGEES recruited staff directly into DPER and subsequently they moved to the Departments on secondment. While this was an efficient model for recruitment in the early stages of IGEES, it had led to several issues. First, it led to a widespread sentiment, that IGEES staff were primarily identified and affiliated with DPER, limiting the ability of IGEES staff to immerse themselves and contribute positively to departments' activities. The new model, where IGEES staff are placed directly in Departments has partly resolved this issue, even if there are still some IGEES members on secondment. While all staff at AO level are on the same pay scale, regardless of what Department they are working in, there is a perception that those working in the DPER are at an advantage when it comes to promotion opportunities and thus have access to higher pay scales at AP and PO levels. A contributory factor to this perception is the fact that in central Departments (PER, Finance and Taoiseach) the grades of AP and PO attract a higher pay scale. This is a function of the grading system in the Irish Civil Service and is not in any way confined or specific to IGEES. There was also an assumption that previous experience in a line department would help for working on DPER votes. While the current structure of the system allows such moves, as it is relatively loose, it does not systematically create expectations that such moves are seen as part of the system.

Overall, these initial recruitment processes tend to form the core of IGEES as a system. Still, as the system is currently maturing, attention also needs to be given to learning and development as well as to managing career opportunities in a broader sense. The extent to which job descriptions are being shared and needs being assessed from a common perspective across the various departments to allocate the IGEES cohorts remains unclear.

Building skills and knowledge: learning and development

IGEES supports capacity building and skills and knowledge development through a range of approaches, including slightly more flexible opportunities for mobility, a learning and development framework. This is complemented with specific learning and development opportunities as well as platform for discussion on analytical outputs and its relevance for policy such as conferences, seminars and policy discussions sessions.

Opportunities for mobility

Incentives towards mobility are encouraged within IGEES with a provision for AOs to move position after a period of two years, either within the Department or between Departments. The purpose of the mobility is to increase experiences and share skills. However, the system has had to evolve, as mentioned above to create increased shared ownership around IGEES, with direct placement of staff within Ministries at the beginning of the career. However, this direct placement of IGEES staff creates a challenge in terms of mobility, because Departments themselves face little incentive to release a member of staff after having trained them for a number of years. In addition, there is a perception of some form of an implicit career premium tends to exist for staff initially starting at DPER. There also appeared to be a mixed understanding of what the current arrangements for the movement of staff was, with differing views about how long IGEES staff should be in Departments before they were moved on to a different Department.

Overall IGEES has offered a wide network for professional growth and mobility opportunities within the Irish civil service. There is also an AP network (AP Forum) meeting 4 times per year.

Given that IGEES open recruitment is currently only focussed on AOs and APs, there are no promotion opportunities at PO level within the IGEES system, which creates incentives for staff to find such promotion opportunities within the system in a broader sense. Such consideration would also need to be contextualised to reflect that a significant number of Principal Officers in the Civil Service hold economics or related training already, which implies that the existing PO cohort might already draw on significant economic expertise, including from IGEES. Furthermore, a number of Departments already have the position of Chief Economist or Head of Research.

The question also remains as to whether or not to structure the analysis or design function within dedicated units within the various departments, which could create issues of legitimacy among the "policy people", who work at the political and administrative interface with implications in terms of credibility and seniority.

Issues of mobility are to be addressed and discussed as part of the internal advisory group. Achieving mobility within a civil service is generally a significant challenge in many countries. Country size may matter, particularly for the smaller countries where the need for specific skills is acutely felt in some of the sectoral ministries. While Ireland seems to be more flexible than some of the Nordic countries, which lack structured mobility streams, it appears that these are not yet fully built as part of the career paths within the civil service. While Ireland is currently implementing a "One Civil Service Scheme", broadening the scope for mobility in structural terms, building and expanding on the IGEES system might offer interesting opportunities. Considerable work has been done on ensuring that the recruitment processes are not gender biased and the gender diversity in the IGEES network reflects the diversity in the graduate pool. IGEES has also been successful in attracting international European talent, which makes it more diverse generally than other parts of the civil service in Ireland. Still, other remaining dimensions of diversity, such as in terms of ethnicity seem to have been less explored compared to other European countries.

Learning and Development Framework

The IGEES Learning and Development (L&D) Framework took effect from the beginning of 2018. Learning and development needs are agreed according to each individual's development needs as well as the business needs of the Department according to the Business Planning and Strategic priorities. The IGEES L&D offer was intended to supplement the L&D already available through existing Departmental and One Learning L&D Frameworks. Following a consultation process, a cluster of skills and competencies specific to IGEES roles was developed (see Figure 2.1).

Figure 2.1. The IGEES Clusters of Skill Needs [pillars of learning]

Policy Analysis & Evaluation Methods	Appraisal Methods	Data & Advanced Quantitative Methods	Application of Economics	Civil Service Competency Skills
Trend Analysis Rationale Efficiency & Inputs Effectiveness & Outputs Outcomes Impact Analysis including counterfactual, social, regional and regulatory	Multicriteria Analysis Cost Benefit Analysis Understanding public sector appraisal frameworks and reviewing business cases	Introduction to Data Analysis Advanced Excel Statistical Programming (Stata, R, etc.) Big Data Econometrics Data identification and gathering Data visualisation Modelling - demographics	Introduction to economics Microeconomics refresher Macroeconomics refresher Introduction to public sector economics	Communicating to non-specialists Project management Promoting evidence based policy

All learning must be practical and case study based. Training modules will be developed to support those new to subject areas and those in need of developing more advanced techniques.

Source: IGEES (2017) Learning and Development Framework 2017-2019. (IGEES, 2017[1]).

The current learning and development offer has contributed positively to the development of specialised skills in the civil service. The induction process for new starters was a good introduction to the civil service. In terms of the learning and development offer available once recruits were in post, the breadth and depth of the offering are positive. There is in general an important effort to coordinate the offer of courses to reduce the scope for duplication. Nevertheless, the offering could be improved. Some popular courses are typically oversubscribed and so finding ways to increase the number of such courses would be desirable. There is scope for further rationalisation of the offering of courses offered within the departments and those offered centrally by IGEES. In order to mainstream such analytic skills across the Irish civil service, the IGEES Unit in DPER delivers modules under the general Civil Service graduate training programme on evidence-based policymaking.

Building capacity for evidence informed policy making goes beyond investing in the skills of IGEES recruits and other skilled policy analysts. It is important for capacity to generate and use evidence for policy making to become a mainstream part of the civil service, which starts but should not stop with IGEES. For example, the Department of Taoiseach has commenced work under the Action 22 of the Civil Service Renewal Plan to strengthen policy making approaches in Ireland and has also produced a Handbook for policy making.[1] Other OECD countries have experience of these twin challenges – trying to mainstream evidence informed policy making across the whole of the civil service whilst simultaneously developing specialist analytical capacity. For example, in New Zealand, the Policy Project sought to build the capacity for evidence informed policy making across the entire civil service Box 2.1.

Box 2.1. Building civil service capacity for EIPM in New Zealand – the Policy Project

The New Zealand Policy Project was launched in 2014 to improve the quality of policy advice being produced across government agencies. It deployed policy analytic tools to investigate current practices in policy design and developed a Policy Skills Framework that makes transparent the evidence, analysis and evaluation skills that are important in a civil servant's skillset. (Acquah, Lisek and Jacobzone, 2019[2]).

A key aim was to ensure that policy advice was developed based on the best available evidence and insights, including an understanding of 'what works'. The government recognised that there was a need to improve the evidence-base of their policy advice and to better design policies and programmes around the needs of users.

This included developing a '**Policy Methods Toolbox**' which is a repository of policy development methods that helps policy practitioners identify and select the right approach for their policy initiative (Washington and Mintrom, 2018[3]):

- The Toolbox includes a variety of resources including tools, guides and case studies. It is divided into four major themes: Start Right, Behavioural Insights, Design Thinking and Public Participation.
- The Toolbox also provides concrete steps and actions that policy makers can take to improve the policy making process through making better use of research and science, using meta-data, feedback loops and input from frontline operational staff and various forms of evaluation.

Source: (Washington and Mintrom, 2018[3]), (Acquah, Lisek and Jacobzone, 2019[2]).

Finally, while the scheme has currently led to a number of strong professionals being hired and dispersed through the departments, it seems that some of the divide between academia and government remains. An IGEES research fund was established in 2017 with the aim to promote Cross-Departmental cooperation on complex policy issues through research. Still, while this initiative is aimed as cross-sectoral issues, the possibilities to develop research within government through PhD in applied economics still appear limited, with very few partnerships with universities and opportunities for IGEES staff to develop at the PhD level[2]. Although not a PhD in applied economics, there is a possibility for a Doctorate in Governance at the Institute of Public Opportunity to synergise structured Doctoral studies with IGEES analytic outputs[3].

Platforms for discussions

Several events are organised under IGEES auspices, including conferences, seminars and policy discussions. These are aimed at high-level policy issues. IGEES organised an annual conference, and thematic seminars, for example on the challenges faced by small advanced economies, on behavioural or tax issues.

These are very important to establish the quality of the brand and create a sense of community and sharing among participating IGEES economists. In addition, IGEES ensures active presence at the Dublin Economic Workshop. The question remains as to whether these efforts could be expanded at the international level, for example through participation in the European Economic Association or the American Economic Association conferences.

Gaps also exist for the junior isolated economists working in the line ministries, who have mentioned the lack of seminars to discuss on going work as a way to receive support from peers on technical issues, which they cannot necessarily receive in their professional environment. Active sharing and collaboration could be encouraged by organising team reviews ("show and tells") where staff members get the opportunity to demonstrate and discuss their work. In the United States, the National Bureau of economic research organises several waves of thematic seminars where PhD Students as well as government economists can present and share on going work. In France, there are several series of annual seminars held on a monthly or biweekly basis (Fourgeaud Economics, INSEE seminars), where government economists can share on going applied analytical work for comment and discussion.

Tools

The role of frameworks and guidelines

Various guidelines have been developed in Ireland for carrying out different aspects of policy analysis. The Irish Government has established the Public Spending Code (PSC), Value for Money and Policy Reviews, Focussed Policy Assessments, a Spending Review, Performance Reporting, as well as Regulatory Impact Assessments, Tax Expenditure Evaluation Guidelines and a Code of Practice for the Governance of State Bodies. The Tax Expenditure Evaluation Guidelines introduced by the Department of Finance in 2014 for instance set out best practices and methodologies for ex ante and ex post evaluation.

The Public Spending Code guidelines has been developed by DEPR and was the main instrument used across the Departments included in the case study. Value for Money Guidelines also sit alongside the Public Spending Code. A Social Impact Framework also sets a methodology that the DPER uses. The IGEES skills are well suited and closely related to the Public Spending Code guidelines.

Strong focus on value for money, cost benefit analysis and spending review

IGEES, alongside the wider systems for policy analysis has made huge strides in increasing capacity to carry out and make use of economic analysis techniques in Ireland, and in particular to support the Spending Review process.

Spending Reviews are designed to inform Government spending allocation and maintenance and have played an important role to make expenditure policy more sustainable. The current rolling three-year Spending Review was announced on Budget day 2016 by the Minister for Finance and Public Expenditure and Reform, and is articulated between IGEES units in all Departments, Votes and the DPER (see Figure 1.1 on the Machinery of government involved in EIPM). During the crisis period, the approach to produce spending reviews consisted in each Department preparing submissions using guidance from the DPER. These central Departments provided a challenge role and sometimes conduct internal reviews, including reviews of horizontal or crosscutting issues. Since 2017, this process is less centralised and concerns more the work of other Departments. Although not a set requirement, this process may identify savings options for the Government and reinforce principles of expenditure efficiency and effectiveness into the wider budget process. The previous Comprehensive Reviews of Expenditure process, on the other hand, necessarily had to identify savings options.

Overall, the process creates a large stock of relevant analysis and evaluations across all Departments and Offices, identifying areas of expenditure requiring ongoing analysis and ensuring that such analysis takes part of the Estimates process. It allows for the systematic examination of existing spending programmes in terms of their effectiveness in meeting policy objectives and allows identifying the need to re-allocate funding to meet expenditure priorities.

Under the Spending Reviews, about 80 papers have been published, covering a wide range of important topics such as, health, education, justice, pay bill expenditure, workforce planning and digitalisation. In addition to improving the deficit position, reviews intend to ensure all expenditure is considered when Government is making budget decisions (Kennedy and Howlin, 2017[4]). While the Spending Reviews provide a useful platform to proliferate IGEES work, it might be useful to consider how to broaden the policy cycle beyond spending reviews and go beyond cost-efficiency and ex ante evaluations for instance.

By nature, the spending review process requires a coordination of expertise from the sectoral spending departments with a review and challenge function by the central departments. The role of IGEES is to ensure that both central and sectoral departments are equipped with appropriate capacity for economic and policy analysis, which is designed to make the process more impactful and more effective. Some recent developments have led to the Spending Reviews becoming a more collaborative process, whilst maintaining DPER's critical challenge function as a finance ministry. Some departments and the Votes within DPER had collaborated on the selection of Spending Review topics. This had helped to make the engagement more productive and useful for both sides. On the other hand, in the Department of Children and Youth Affairs, only the Vote Section chose topics for both 2018 and 2019.

There were also examples of joint analysis both within and outside of the context of the Spending Review, which are a useful way of pooling expertise and bringing together different perspectives on the same problem, which was greatly helped by the distribution and sharing of IGEES staffing resources.

Broadening the analytical framework beyond the spending code and strict VFM approaches

Spending code guidelines may not capture all the dimensions that are relevant for policy evaluation, due to their strict focus on expenditure and value for money. Some Departments have also developed frameworks to support their own activity in particular areas. The Department of Business, Enterprise and Innovation (DBEI) has developed a robust framework for evaluation specifically in relation to enterprise support programmes. DBEI developed the framework based on a review of international best practice in enterprise evaluation. International experience confirms that guidelines for carrying out different elements of policy analysis can be a key component of improving the quality of policy analysis and evaluation (OECD, 2020[5]).

Most OECD countries tend to use some form of a guide for policy evaluation within government. Given the increasing focus on outcomes as well as on wellbeing in supporting policy priorities across a range of OECD countries, it is also important that such instruments can also support a focus on result, and be flexible enough to capture a broad range of policy outcomes. For example in Ireland, while the department of health mobilises some tools for economic analysis, it also develops broader frameworks for understanding the impact of health policy and resources on people, which requires attention to the many determinants of health status that are beyond the realm of the health care system itself. Canada has developed a range of frameworks and guidelines that cover several aspects of evaluation (see Box 2.2).

> **Box 2.2. The role of frameworks and guidelines for the promotion of EIPM in Canada**
>
> **Evaluation in the Government of Canada**
>
> The Results Division of the Canadian Secretariat, successor of the Centre of Excellence (CEE) for Evaluation, is responsible for evaluation activities within the Government of Canada. It offers useful resources, information and tools for Government professionals and anyone interested in evaluation at the federal level. Moreover, requirements for evaluation practices are outlined in the *Policy on Result*, which took effect in 2016. Overall, the Secretariat has functional leadership regarding the implementation, use and development of evaluation practices across government. To support quality EIPM, the Treasury Board Secretariat offers a number of useful guidelines:
>
> - **Guide to Rapid Impact Evaluation (RIE) (2017):** this practical guide gives a range of methods for conducting RIE and advice on when and how these can be used in government. More precisely, it defines RIE, the time and resources needed to conduct one, its key benefits and challenges, and support for planning, analysis and reporting the results.
> - **Assessing Program Resource Utilization When Evaluating Federal Programs (2013):** this document is made for evaluators of federal government programmes, programme and financial managers, and corporate planners. It helps them understand, plan and undertake evaluations that include the assessment of resource utilization. It provides them with methodological support to ensure that they have the knowledge and competencies to conduct quality and credible programme resource utilization assessments.
> - **Theory-Based Approaches to Evaluation: Concepts and Practices (2012):** this document introduces key concepts of theory-based approaches to evaluation and their application to federal programmes. It should be complemented by additional readings and advice for step-by-step guidance on conducting evaluations.
> - **Supporting Effective Evaluations: A Guide to Developing Performance Measurement Strategies (2010):** this guide supports departments, programme managers and heads of evaluation in developing performance measurement to support evaluation activities. It provides recommendations, tools and frameworks for conducting clear and concise performance measurement strategies as well as guidance regarding the roles of those in charge of developing such strategies.
>
> Sources: Based on Treasury Board of Canada, 2019[3], 2017[4], 2013[5], 2012[6], 2010[7].

Processes

The department work programmes for policy analysis

Departments varied in the extent to which they decided and formalised their work programme for policy analysis. Some departments had a structured process for determining the work programme, which could include consulting with relevant stakeholders, consideration of the programme for government and considerations of existing and expected future resources. For example, in one department, the specialist unit for policy analysis led the development of the work programme. The unit conducted a range of consultation meetings with divisions across the Department as well as with other stakeholders. Assistant Secretaries then discussed and prioritised a range of options to take forward. The unit then developed these options into a work programme proposed to the Department's management board, who make the final decisions on the work programme. The analysis work specified in the work programme was typically organised into two cycles. The first half of the year focused on planning the analysis and building the evidence base, while the second half of the year was devoted to analysing the evidence base and making policy focused recommendations. These sound arrangements ensure that the scarce IGEES and other human resources are being applied in a way that is well prioritised and avoids fragmentation and lack of structural attention due to constantly shifting short-term political demands.

In many other Departments, a less structured process for deciding policy analysis was the norm. Similarly not all Departments developed a formal work programme for analysis. This was typically the case in Departments with more limited analytical capacity – in terms of numbers of analysts – and in Departments where analysts worked in policy units, in which case the allocation of policy analysis was incorporated into the planning process for the policy unit. An absence of a formal work programme specifically devoted to policy analysis may result in the fact that IGEES staff would not necessarily be able to fully apply their analytical skills. Especially at the AO grade we were told that it could be challenging to protect time spent on the analysis in face of the pressures to manage the day to day of core civil service tasks such as ministerial briefings and responding to parliamentary questions. The challenge is to find a balance between responsiveness to political demands through ensuring that IGEES capacity is immersed in the policy clusters in the ministries, while ensuring the possibility to develop sound analytical products that can take advantage to the proximity of data to improve policy effectiveness.

The balance of work conducted internally versus externally

There was also wide variation between Departments in terms of how analytical resources were allocated and the balance of work done in house and work contracted out externally. Some larger Departments were able to draw on sufficient policy analysis resources internally to be able to complete the majority of the departmental work programme analysis in house. The far more common model was to have a mixture of policy analysis projects conducted in house and contracted externally.

The decision about whether to do policy analysis in house or externally involved a range of considerations including the skills and expertise available in house, the scale of the project, the timeframe for completion and any budgetary constraints. There was no one size fits all solution. There is a range of risks and issues with conducting work in house and contracting it out. When time is a critical factor, there is a tendency to commission out the work to an organisation who would be able to delivery quickly. Commissioning work externally also has the advantage of being somewhat protected from shifting priorities and a change in the availability of policy analysis available in house.

Research commissioning is a complex and specialist exercise that is subject to many risks. There can be challenges when an evaluation is externally commissioned, but where the in house analysts hold the relevant data sets and knowledge of its strengths and limitations for policy analysis. This situation requires sufficient time and resource so that the in house team can hand over and explain the data to the contractor. This situation can present resource challenges if the in house analysts are working on activities that are more urgent. Another issue that came up relatively frequently was ensuring that sufficient internal policy analysis capacity could be devoted to the commissioning process itself. In some Departments, every policy analysis project that is commissioned by the Department must go through the specialised unit for policy analysis. This has several advantages. First, it means that the in house analysts can take a decision about whether an existing policy analysis project fulfils the requirement. If not a decision can then be made, about whether there is the competency and capacity to do the work internally or whether it is necessary for it to be commissioned externally. Additionally, this ensures that findings from commissioned work can be interpreted, communicated and absorbed internally. Another advantage is that the analyst can act as a broker between the policy teams and the external contractor. This ensures that the invitation to tender clearly and accurately specifies the nature of the policy analysis. It also ultimately increases the likelihood of an appropriate and high quality project given the policy concern.

References

Acquah, D., K. Lisek and S. Jacobzone (2019), "The Role of Evidence Informed Policy Making in Delivering on Performance: Social Investment in New Zealand", https://www.oecd-ilibrary.org/docserver/74fa8447-en.pdf?expires=1568195730&id=id&accname=ocid84004878&checksum=44215ED1C60EC9362961EFE7B4B79984 (accessed on 11 September 2019). [2]

IGEES (2017), *IGEES Learning & Development Framework 2017-2019*, https://igees.gov.ie/wp-content/uploads/2017/12/IGEES-Learning-and-Development-Framework-2017-19-For-Launch.pdf (accessed on 12 August 2019). [1]

Kennedy, F. and J. Howlin (2017), "Spending reviews in Ireland-Learning from experience", *OECD Journal on Budgeting*, Vol. 2016/2, pp. 93-109, https://www.oecd-ilibrary.org/docserver/budget-16-5jg30cchf0g0.pdf?expires=1565605875&id=id&accname=ocid84004878&checksum=53F7E58BBFC1BEF3E24DE76EFFB045D9 (accessed on 12 August 2019). [4]

OECD (2020), *Institutionalisation, Quality and Use of Policy Evaluation, Governance Lessons from countries experience, forthcoming*. [5]

Washington, S. and M. Mintrom (2018), "Strengthening policy capability: New Zealand's Policy Project", http://dx.doi.org/10.1080/25741292.2018.1425086 (accessed on 11 September 2019). [3]

Notes

[1] The Action 22 is about Strengthen policy-making skills and develop more open approaches to policy-making. See https://www.gov.ie/en/policy-information/fd9c03-civil-service-renewal/?referrer=/en/civil-service-renewal/.

[2] IGEES staff do have the opportunity to apply for funding to support academic study through the Refund of Fees Scheme within Departments.

[3] https://www.ipa.ie/audit-and-governance/doctorate-in-governance-dgov.2049.html.

3 Overall effectiveness of IGEES and areas for further investment

This chapter discusses the remaining barriers to evidence informed policy making, including data availability and use, as well as recruitment and retention of staff. The chapter highlights opportunities to strengthen the full range of policy analysis, the options for strengthening capacity for social research and for evidence synthesis. The chapter offers options for moving from knowledge management to knowledge brokerage to build the use of results into policymaking as well as for strengthening communications and branding.

Remaining barriers to evidence informed policy making

While this section highlights a number of remaining challenges, this should not obscure the fact that overall the general impression is that IGEES has made a significant difference and that progress is being achieved in many areas in strengthening capacity for policy making. As a successful small open economy, Ireland does not seem to be facing some of structural challenges that are faced in some of the larger neighbouring countries, namely the lack of trust, the perceived impartiality of the civil service, and preserving the political/administrative interface. The level of trust, the recognised professional skills in the civil service and a functioning political administrative interface, still appear to remain structural characteristics of the Irish systems. Still, some of the pressures remain, and the management and rationalisation of choices for major public infrastructure projects still present significant challenges at time.

Data availability and use

Progress towards evidence informed policy making is hampered by the availability of adequate data and the Department's capacity to use it in Ireland, as is the case in many OECD countries. In some cases, the challenge was to understand what data and data sets currently existed within departments, and how departments could use the data for policy analysis providing adequate incentives to data producers. Some departments had created a 'Data Map', setting out the relevant departmental and agency data to increase awareness of the data that is held by the policy units. Other departments were still in the process of building up their departmental data infrastructure, which needed dedicated analytical resource to be effective. Departments that worked with agencies and arm's length bodies faced particular challenges in data access because these Departments were not typically the 'owner' of much of the data and evidence needed to carry out policy analysis. The sharing of data across departments also seemed to represent very significant challenges.

There were also a number of challenges in making full use of the available data. There is some concern about using individual level data to evaluate policies and programmes, with data protection issues assumed to be an obstacle. Academics spoke of their frustration at the complexity of the processes they were required to go through for even repeat requests to use the same data sets of multiple occasions. It also seems that existing government's IT systems are facing limitations, resulting in challenges to carry out statistical and other forms of analysis. Given the achievements and progress that the Irish government is making in terms of improving data infrastructures, IGEES should consider the opportunity of better inscribing its work within the broader data-driven public sector strategies of the country, by collaborating or aligning agendas with digital government teams for instance.

While IGEES has been meant as a scheme to strengthen capacity for rigorous economic evaluation through an investment in skills, it has not been broadly associated with a strategy to strengthen evidence and promote smart data, which would have more systematically linked with the statistical side and have fostered systematic access to administrative data. Some other countries, such as the US and Japan are now implementing more systematic approaches to implement an evidence-based policy making agenda, with institutional resources, promoting internal champions and exploring the possibility to fully use existing data on a more systematic basis (See Box 3.1. and Box 3.2 for US and Japan EBPM initiatives).

> **Box 3.1. Building the foundations for evidence-based policymaking in the US**
>
> For federal agencies to better acquire, access, and use evidence to inform decision-making, the Evidence Act was signed into law on January 14th, 2019. This Act mandates evidence-generating activities across agencies, open government data, confidential information protection, as well as skills and capacity building. It also includes provisions for appointing a Chief Data Officer (CDO) by each agency and establishing a CDO council. (Office of Management and Budget, 2018[1])
>
> The Evidence Act requires agencies to designate an **Evaluation Officer**, which strengthens an agency's capacity to build evidence. Senior evaluation officials are responsible for coordinating the agency's evaluation activities, learning agenda and information reported to the Office of Management and Budget (OMB) on evidence. They also have to establish and use multi-year learning agendas, document the resources dedicated to program evaluation, and finally improve the quality of the information provided to OMB on evidence-building activities. (OECD, 2018[2])
>
> Precisely, the multi-year learning agendas allow agencies to identify and address policy questions and include operational and strategic questions concerning agencies' human resources, internal processes, etc. The evidence-building plans include the policy questions that the agency intends to answer, the data needed, and the challenges faced in generating evidence to support policymaking. (Office of Management and Budget, 2019[3])
>
> Additionally, the OMB has a dedicated **Evidence Team** that works with other OMB offices in order to set research priorities and ensure the use of appropriate evaluation methodologies in federal evaluations. Interestingly, as of July 2019, the team will create and coordinate an interagency council that regroups Evaluation Officers. This council will serve as a forum to exchange information and advise the OMB on issues affecting the evaluation functions such as evaluator competencies, best practices for programme evaluation, and capacity building. The council will also allow coordination and collaboration between evaluators and the government and will play a leadership role for the larger Federal evaluation community. To ensure evidence is used in policy design, the Evidence Team is also actively involved offering technical assistance to Federal Agencies. (Clark, 2019[4])
>
> Sources: (Office of Management and Budget, 2018[1]), (OECD, 2018[2]), (Office of Management and Budget, 2019[3]), (Clark, 2019[4]).

> **Box 3.2. Institutionalisation of Policy Evaluation in Japan**
>
> To provide the Japanese policy evaluation system with a clear-cut framework and improve its effectiveness, Japan has enacted **The Government Policy Evaluations Act of 2001.** It enunciates the obligation of each ministry to evaluate adopted policies and specifies detailed steps for evaluation processes conducted by the Ministry of Internal Affairs and Communications (MIC).
>
> Following the Act, the Japanese Cabinet created "**Basic Guidelines for Implementing Policy Evaluation**", which offer advice to facilitate planned and steady policy evaluation across government. Each ministry thereby determines a "Basic Plan for Policy Evaluation," over 3 to 5-year periods to incorporate policy evaluation into the policy management cycle. Under the basic plan, each ministry should also determine an "Implementation Plan for Policy Evaluation", which is a 1-year plan that is revised after expiration. This plan specifies the policies to be evaluated in the year and how they should be implemented (Japanese Cabinet, 2017[5]).

> Under the Act, the **Administrative Evaluation Bureau** (AEB) of the MIC formulates guidelines for implementing policy evaluations, aggregates all policy evaluation reports across the government, and conducts reviews to improve the quality of those evaluations (The Ministry of Internal Affairs and Communications, 2012[6]). From FY2012, the AEB introduced a standard format for ex-post evaluations reports, which made them more easily understood and shared across ministries. Besides, the AEB set up a portal site for policy evaluation that provides links to policy evaluation data including analysis sheets and evaluation reports publicized by each ministry to ensure transparency and accountability (The Ministry of Internal Affairs and Communications, 2010[7]).
>
> Moreover, to promote EPBM practices across government, the Statistics Reform Promotion Council was established in the Prime Minister's office in 2017. This entailed setting up a new Director-General (DG) for Evidence-Based Policymaking in each ministry and ensuring that these EBPM DGs work together across government (The Statistical Reform Promotion Council, 2017[8]).
>
> The Committee on Promoting EBPM, which includes the responsible DGs, developed "Policy on Recruitment and Capacity Building of Human Resources to Promote EBPM ". The government thereby addresses public relations related to EBPM by holding cross-ministerial training and studying sessions (The Committee on Promoting EBPM, 2017[9]).
>
> Besides, ministries practice trial EBPM (where they identify problems, set objectives, predict and measure effects) and use the results for changing and making policies. Ministries have to report on their EBPM trials to the Committee. The AEB of the MIC also implements EBPM in joint empirical studies with line ministries (The Cabinet Secretariat, 2019[10]).
>
> Sources: (Japanese Cabinet, 2017[5]), (The Ministry of Internal Affairs and Communications, 2012[6]), (The Ministry of Internal Affairs and Communications, 2010[7]), (The Statistical Reform Promotion Council, 2017[8]), (The Committee on Promoting EBPM, 2017[9]), (The Cabinet Secretariat, 2019[10]) (in Japanese).

All of the abovementioned challenges also point to the need of building solid data governance foundations supporting the use of evidence in decision-making. This would contribute to enhancing coherent implementation and coordination, and strengthening the institutional, regulatory, capacity and technical foundations to better control and manage the data value cycle, *i.e.* collect, generate, store, secure, process, share, and re-use data, as means to enhance trust and deliver value (OECD, *2019*).

In light of the above, data sharing tools such as data infrastructures or the use of APIs and open data towards greater data sharing, should complement the more tactical and strategic elements relevant of data governance (see Figure 3.1) from data stewardship to public sector capacity and the enabling regulatory frameworks (e.g. for data sharing). It might be useful to consider how to coordinate the need for evidence and economic analysis with the data governance agenda, as is the case for example in the US through the implementation of the "Evidence Informed Policy Making" Act. It is important to avoid fragmentation and duplication of efforts (e.g. in developing separate data sharing infrastructures), and to promote public sector integration and cohesion.

Figure 3.1. Data governance in the public sector

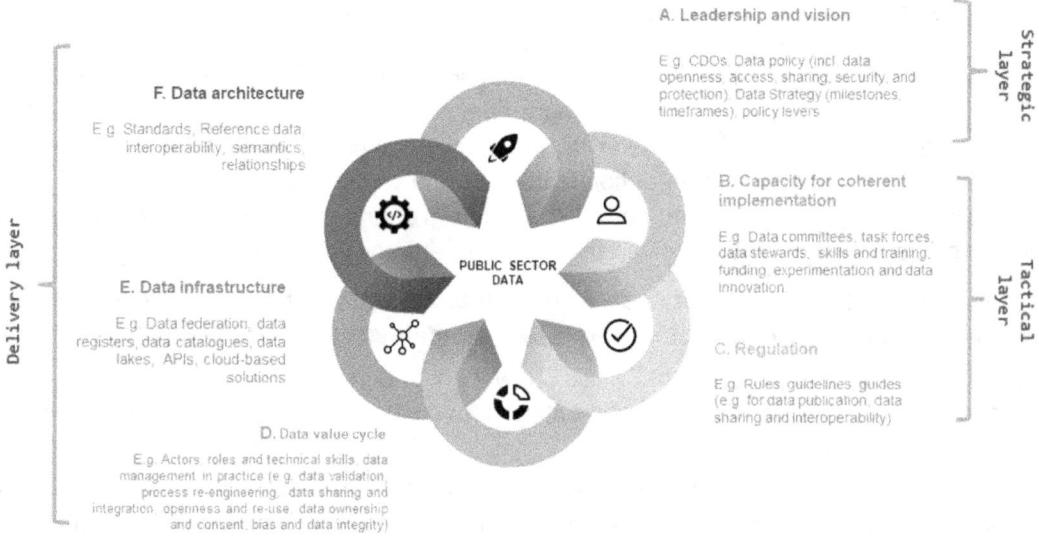

Source: (OECD, 2019[11]).

Recruitment and retention of staff

The robust jobs market in Ireland means that IGEES competes with a diverse range of public and private sector organisations to recruit from a relatively small pool of graduate economists. The variety of job positions offered, the quality of analytical work and the possibility of internal mobility were signalled as strong assets that motivate candidates to apply for IGEES jobs. Departments were unanimously positive about IGEES having broadened up the recruitment to other graduates with relevant policy analysis skills such as social scientists. It appears desirable to continue the process of diversifying the pool of entrants. Many departments still have capacity gaps, with only a small number of analysts to service the policy analysis needs of the entire department. It is also necessary to build a critical mass of analysts in departments in order for the policy analysis function to truly realise its potential, which is the case in only part of the departments surveyed. While retention of analysts is not generally seen as a major challenge, the fact is that many analysts are also finding career paths elsewhere inside the civil service in some more managerial positions.

While the focus on strengthening provision of analytical capacity at the Administrative Officer and Assistant Principal is a core asset of IGEES, an open question remains about whether further developments should continue with the Principal Officer (PO) grade. Currently, there are no formally designated IGEES staff at PO grade, although there are cases where departments had badged roles such as 'Chief Economist. This might affect the career prospects of some IGEES recruits, notably those less willing to progress into generalist positions.

However, such issues for leadership in analytical jobs should not only be seen from the perspective of internal IGEES management, but also as opportunities to create "champions" for an evidence and economic evaluation agenda within government, in a way that would be clearly recognisable, and also identified as such up to the political level. Some other countries have designated positions such as "Chief Economist", "Chief Statisticians", or Chief scientist, Chief Evaluator such as the UK, Canada, the US or France. This is also a way to signal the importance of such evidence driven tasks within governments, and the fact that the post holders for such positions should also be seen as a source for authoritative advice, among both citizens and politicians.

Overall effectiveness and key areas for further investment

IGEES as a capacity building initiative within the Civil Service

There is no doubt that IGEES has been successful in building capacity for evidence informed policy making in Ireland. These efforts will need to continue over a number of years. It is also critical that IGEES initiatives connect with government wide initiatives such as the Public Service Reform Plan (PSRP). In OECD's assessment of the PSRP a key recommendation is that in order to meet its objectives a careful look at the skills and capabilities is required in order to deliver the required changes in Ireland's civil and public service – and a number of the question keys identified in that report are still pertinent:

- What are the current skills and/or capacity gaps that are limiting the successful implementation of reform? What are the priority sectors and levels for addressing these gaps?
- Beyond technical and professional skills, how can the Irish public service foster risk taking, evaluation and learning (through experimentation, evaluation, etc.) to support innovation and build learning organisations?
- While the PSRP has developed additional capacity (PMOs, economic analysis for example), how can it ensure that it leverages organisational change throughout ministries and agencies so that there is broad ownership of the reform process and results?

OECD's work on Building Capacity for Evidence Informed Policy Making (REF) would provide useful material for Ireland to make a more in depth assessment of the strengths and weaknesses across the different dimensions of EIPM. Six skills clusters are identified which could be used to identify skill and capacity gaps that continue to impede EIPM.

Opportunities to strengthen the full range of policy analysis

IGEES has built up strengths in core economic analysis over the medium term, but in the longer term the full range of policy analysis tools need mainstreaming throughout the system. Key areas for focus include developing and mainstreaming skills for impact evaluation, for evidence synthesis and for wider social research.

Strengthening capacity for impact evaluation

The assessment reveals a need to develop capacity for impact evaluation. Sometimes referred to 'counterfactual impact evaluation' such studies typically privilege internal validity, which pertains to inferences about whether the observed correlation between the intervention and outcomes reflect an underlying causal relationship. Determining the efficacy of an intervention is a complex process, involving considerations on the evaluation design, sample, measurements, methods of analysis, and findings. A range of different evaluation designs can establish the efficacy of a policy or programmes including both experimental and quasi-experimental approaches (see Box 3.3).

> **Box 3.3. Standards for establishing the efficacy of an intervention**
>
> The What Works Centre for Local Economic Growth (WWG) is an independent organisation from the UK, mainly, focus on producing systematic reviews of the evidence on a broad range of policies in the area of local economic growth.
>
> WWG assessment is based on the Maryland Scientific Methods Scale (SMS), which ranks policy evaluations from 1 (least robust: studies based on simple cross sectional correlations) to 5 (most robust: Randomised Control Trials.). The ranking aims to present the extent to which the methods deal with the selection biases inherent to policy evaluations (robustness), and the quality of its implementation to achieve efficacy, as following:
>
> - Level 2: Use of adequate control variables and either (a) a cross-sectional comparison of treated groups with untreated groups, or (b) a before-and-after comparison of treated group, without an untreated comparison group.
> - Level 3: Comparison of outcomes in treated group after an intervention, with outcomes in the treated group before the intervention, and a comparison group used to provide a counterfactual (e.g. difference in difference). Techniques such as regression and propensity score matching may be used to adjust for difference between treated and untreated groups, but there are likely to be important unobserved differences remaining.
> - Level 4: Quasi-randomness in treatment is exploited, so that it can be credibly held that treatment and control groups differ only in their exposure to the random allocation of treatment. This often entails the use of an instrument or discontinuity in treatment, the suitability of which should be adequately demonstrated and defended.
> - Level 5: Reserved for research designs with Randomised Control Trials (RCTs) providing the definitive example. Extensive evidence provided on comparability of treatment and control groups, showing no significant differences in terms of levels or trends. Additionally. Attention paid to problems of selective attrition, and there should be limited or, ideally, no occurrence of 'contamination' of the control group with the treatment.
>
> Source: What Works Centre for Local Economic Growth ([100]).

Although there were some examples of high quality impact evaluation from a number Departments, overall impact evaluation is still a rarity in the Irish government. Strengthening Ireland's data infrastructure will increase the opportunities to carry out impact evaluations using quasi-experimental methods based on existing administrative data (see above). Although experimental approaches, such as randomised control trials, can sometimes take advantage of existing administrative data, it is often necessary to collect new data using social research methods. Developing capacity for social research is another area where IGEES can focus over the longer term, including through leveraging its research funds (see next section).

A focus on developing theories of change and logic models can improve the quality of both policy design and impact evaluation. A theory of change can be defined as set of interrelated assumptions explaining how and why an intervention is likely to produce outcomes in the target population (European Monitoring Centre for Drugs and Drug Addiction, 2011[12]). Engaging in the process of developing a theory of change leads to better policy planning, implementation, and monitoring because the policy or programme activities are linked to a detailed and plausible understanding of how change actually happens. A logic model sets out the conceptual connections between concepts in the theory of change to show what intervention, at what intensity, delivered to whom and at what intervals would likely produce specified short term, intermediate and long term outcomes (Axford et al., 2005[13]; Epstein and Klerman, 2012[14]). A logic model is a critical tool to allow detailed coherent and realistic policy planning. A full list of the benefits of developing both a theory of change and logic model in reproduced in Box 3.4.

> **Box 3.4. The benefits of developing an intervention theory of change and logic model**
>
> 1. The evaluability of the programme—for both implementation and outcomes—is facilitated, by signposting appropriate metrics.
> 2. The original intentions of the programme developers are clearly set out, and are explicit and open to critique.
> 3. The underlying logic of the assumptions made in the theory, for example, that undertaking a certain activity will lead to a particular outcome, can be scrutinised.
> 4. The realism of the assumptions made by the programme developers can be checked against wider evidence of 'what works', to assess the likelihood of the programme being successful.
> 5. Commissioners can check the programme meets their needs; and providers and practitioners delivering the programme can check their own assumptions and the alignment of their expectations against the original intentions of the programme developers.

In addition, scope might exist to expand the role of IGEES in developing professional approaches to equality-related analysis. For instance, operational tools for equality budgeting could be developed, expanding beyond the performance-budgeting foundation in which Ireland already has significant strengths. The (Forthcoming) OECD Equality Budget Scan of Ireland precisely suggests that *ex ante* assessments of policy areas such as poverty and its intersection with various equality dimensions should be complemented by *ex post* equality impact assessment, to track whether policies are meeting equality objectives and if they have equality-related impacts. In particular, equality-related analysis could be integrated in a systematic and structured manner in the Spending Review process.

Developing such tools may require developing additional tools to those already available, such as the Public Spending Code and other frameworks, as well as actively promoting some of the existing cases of impact evaluation in order to emulate change and provide incentives towards greater adoption of such approaches. More precisely, the Public Spending Code is a set of procedures and rules that ensures that value-for-money is obtained in public spending. A key portion of the Code is devoted to developing theories of change and logic models (Department of Public Expenditure and Reform, 2019[15]). To assess expenditure programmes, two main methodologies used across the Irish civil service are the Value for Money Reviews (VFMRs) and Focused Policy Assessments (FPAs). The former consists in the evaluation or major spending programmes or specific policies, while the latter is an evaluation methodology specifically related to policy configuration and delivery (IGEES, 2018[16]). Still within the scope of government spending and impact evaluation, the Department of the Taoiseach provided guidelines on conducting regulatory impact analysis (Department of the Taoiseach, 2009[17]), which now sit with DPER as part of the Public Spending Code. The Department of Finance provides guidelines specifically targeted at the evaluation of tax expenditure (Department of Finance, 2014[18]). The latter sets best practices for ex ante and ex post evaluation of tax expenditure.

As such, the currently existing tools have a major focus on value-for-money and optimising government spending. Although of incontestable value, this approach lacks a broader perspective on well-being and inclusive growth, which could be supported by the development of appropriate analytic tools. Such instruments have been developed in countries such as Scotland and New Zealand, which shows policy frameworks that address wellbeing and inequalities, in line with economic development (See Box 3.6 on Approaches to well-being for policy making in Scotland).

Strengthening capacity for social research

IGEES was already making progress in augmenting capacity for social research. As with impact evaluation, whilst there were many high quality examples of social research across the Irish government, overall the government has not well institutionalised social research methods. The comparison with a country with a Government Social Research (GSR) profession such as the UK is informative (See Box 3.5). This is due to the origins of IGEES, which has developed in the aftermath of the global financial crisis, to strengthen capacity for sound expenditure management.

Box 3.5. The UK Government Social Research Profession

The GSR profession is one of the Civil Service Professions that works alongside other analysts (economists, statisticians and operational researchers). GSR professionals use the core methods of social scientific enquiry, such as surveys, controlled trials, qualitative research, case studies and analysis of administrative and statistical data in order to explain and predict social and economic phenomena for policymaking.

Members of the GSR profession come from a wide variety of social science backgrounds, including candidates with degrees in psychology, geography, sociology and criminology. The GSR profession has its own competency framework that begins with entry-level graduates as part of the fast stream to members of the senior civil service and most UK government departments would have a Chief Social Researcher who leads and supports the activity of social researchers within the department.

Source: UK Government, "Government Social Research Profession". Accessed 2 September 2019.
https://www.gov.uk/government/organisations/civil-service-government-social-research-profession/about.

Such broadening of the capacity of social research might also be facilitated by some slight adjustment of focus, for example with increased attention to well-being outcomes, in line with international trends (see Box 3.6 and example of Scotland).

> **Box 3.6. Approaches to Well-Being for policymaking in Scotland**
>
> Scotland's **National Performance Framework** (NPF) represents an instructive experience on the promotion of government accountability for inclusive growth with a well-being perspective. This Framework involves a co-ordination mechanism that ensures alignment of strategies and programmes across sectors, in support of broader national outcomes. It sets out a wide range of indicators (81 as of September 2019) against which the progress of the Scottish government is measured and reported on a publicly accessible website. The indicators measure national and societal wellbeing, incorporating economic, social and environmental targets that are updated with available data. (Scottish Government, 2019[19]).
>
> Precisely, these targets relate to business, employment, education and skills, child well-being, health, inequalities, social exclusion, safety, sustainable consumption, etc., which goes beyond traditional measures of GDP. These indicators were built on public consultations, through extensive surveys and workshop across the country involving diverse social groups. Moreover, Scottish Ministers have a duty to consult on, develop and publish a new set of National Outcomes for Scotland, and to review them at least every five years (Acquah, Lisek and Jacobzone, 2019[20]).
>
> Such outcomes-based framework enables translating inclusive and well-being goals into reality, by selecting specific policy interventions based on evidence and aligning high-level goals onto budgetary allocations and other policy interventions (OECD, 2016[21]). Some Departments within the Scottish Government, such as the Department of Justice, has shown great success in linking the targets and outcomes of the NPF to their strategic actions and decision-making. The full achievement of well-being outcomes requires overcoming the remaining challenge of incorporating the NPF into government's actions and spending programmes.
>
> Source: (OECD, 2016[21]), (Scottish Government, 2019[19]), (Acquah, Lisek and Jacobzone, 2019[20]).

Strengthening capacity for evidence synthesis

Evidence synthesis is another area that would benefit from development in Ireland, particularly through increased knowledge management at the level of the various analytical units. Evidence syntheses, through secondary processing of existing studies, provide a vital tool for policy makers and practitioners to find what works, how it works – and what might do harm, often at a cost that is lower than that of conducting one new evaluation. . Evidence syntheses are also critical in informing what is not known from previous research. As the number of studies increases, it becomes more difficult for policy makers and practitioners to keep abreast of the literature. Furthermore, policies should ideally be based on assessed of the body of evidence, not single studies, which may not provide a full picture of the effectiveness of a policy or programme. This need to draw on bodies of evidence has led to an increase in the use of evidence synthesis.

Whilst there were a small number of Departments already engaged in evidence synthesis, overall knowledge of the different forms of evidence synthesis was at the early stages in Ireland and most of the evidence synthesis was restricted to literature reviews. Although literature reviews can be useful for providing information on a topic in a short period, literature reviews have a number of serious weaknesses. Literature reviews are prone to selection and publication bias and because they are often unclear on their methodology, assessing the strength of the conclusions is challenging. To overcome these and other challenges, more formal and transparent methodologies for evidence synthesis have been developed, including quick scoping reviews, rapid evidence assessments and systematic reviews (See Box 3.7).

> **Box 3.7. Different methodologies for reviewing the evidence base**
>
> Effective policymaking requires using the best available evidence, which itself requires reviewing and choosing from the already existing evidence on the policy question. Different reviewing methods enable managing and interpreting the results of this large evidence base:
>
> - Quick Scoping Review: this non-systematic method can take from 1 week to 2 months. It consists in doing a quick overview of the available research on a specific topic to determine the range of existing studies on the topic. It allows mapping the literature concerning a delimited question by using only easily accessible, electronic and key resources, going up to two bibliographical references.
> - Rapid Evidence Assessment (REA): this systematic and more time-consuming method (2 to 6 months) consists in quickly overviewing the existing research on a specific policy issue and synthesising the evidence provided by this research. It intends to rigorously and explicitly search, and critically appraise this evidence. To gain time, it may limit certain aspects of the systematic review process, such as narrowing the REA question or the type and breadth of data considered. Shortening the traditional systematic review process provides a rapid synthesis of the existing relevant evidence, but suffers the risk of introducing bias.
> - Systematic Review: this is the most robust method for reviewing, synthesising and mapping existing evidence on a particular policy topic. It is more resource-intensive, as it can take up to 8 to 12 months minimum and requires a researcher team. It has explicit objectives and a thorough search strategy that considers a broad range of data. Studies are chosen and screened according to explicit and uniform criteria, and reasons for excluding certain studies have to be stated. This transparent and comprehensive method maximally reduces bias in the search, choice and synthesis of the existing research. Moreover, it allows the creation of a cumulative and sound evidence base on a specific policy subject. Lastly, systematic reviews are applicable to quantitative studies as well as other types of questions.
>
> Source: The UK Civil Service, *What is a Rapid Evidence Assessment?* https://webarchive.nationalarchives.gov.uk/20140402163359/http://www.civilservice.gov.uk/networks/gsr/resources-and-guidance/rapid-evidence-assessment/what-is (Accessed 12 August 2019).

Developing capacity to carry out full systematic reviews, which can take up to two years, is beyond the scope of all but the most analytically well-resourced Departments. Fortunately, there exist a number of high-quality databases of existing systematic reviews such as Cochrane, Campbell and the UK What Works Centres. These resources could become more integral resources that Departments consider during the policy design phase of any new proposal. There is scope for integrating such approaches more broadly in the Irish system, in a way that could be facilitated by IGEES tools and resources, including dissemination seminars.

Building the use of results into decision making

OECD's review of Ireland's Public Service Reform Plan concluded that whilst building evaluation and experimentation processes into policymaking is an important first step, a further challenge is to ensure that the results get used in decision-making. This is a common challenge that governments face: despite an increase in policy analysis and the potential for policies to be based on evidence, in reality an effective connection with many types of evidence in policymaking can be elusive.

Moving from knowledge management to knowledge brokerage

In terms of knowledge management, most Departments attempted to publish the majority of reports on their website. Ireland could consider moving beyond these strategies aimed at pushing research at policymakers and instead develop strategies to build the demand for evidence. Some departments had already developed strategies to encourage interaction between analysts and policy makers. Strategic policy discussions, policy forums and presentations are some of the examples of activities Departments had engaged in to stimulate demand for evidence. Across OECD countries, governments have also invested in structured and long term approaches to building demand. In Australia, the Policy Liaison Initiative was an attempt to improve the use of evidence synthesis. This involved creating an 'Evidence-Based Policy Network' to facilitate knowledge sharing between policy makers and researchers, alongside seminars by national and international researchers in field of evidence synthesis and implementation (see Box 3.8). The current framework of IGEES related events provides an opportunity to develop such approaches.

Box 3.8. The Policy Liaison Initiative for improving the use of Cochrane systematic reviews

The Policy Liaison Initiative (PLI) is a long-term knowledge translation initiative designed to support the use of Cochrane systematic reviews in health policy. A joint initiative between the Australasian Cochrane Centre and Australian Government Department of Health and Ageing, the PLI includes three core elements.

1. *A community of practice for evidence-informed policy.* This comprised of an Evidence- Based Policy Network to facilitate knowledge sharing between policy makers and the Cochrane Collaboration. The members of the network receive bulletins alerting them to new and updated reviews. Seminars by national and international researchers in field of evidence synthesis and implementation were also provided.

2. *Skills building workshops.* These covered a range of topics including types of evidence, research study design and matching, searching for empirical and review evidence, critical appraisal and applying evidence to the local context. The training material and resources from the workshops were made available on the website.

3. *A website and summaries of policy relevant reviews.* A web portal for indexing and accessing policy relevant Cochrane reviews and summaries was created. A tailored summary format was also created to present the findings of reviews.

Source: Adapted from (Brennan et al., 2016[22]).

Other interventions adopt more structured approaches to bring policy makers into contact with individual scientists, through collaborating in the development of research projects as well as ad-hoc or formalised systems of parliamentary advice where researchers are called to provide advice. In 2015, the UK Cabinet Office set up the 'Cross-Government Trial Advice Panel' in partnership with the Economic and Social Research Council. The Trial Advice Panel brings together a team of experts from academia and within the civil service to support the use of experiments in public policy (What Works Network, 2018[23]). It also offers a means of combining expertise, allowing departments with limited expertise in evaluation to work with departments that do, as well top academic experts. In so doing, the Trial Advice Panel aims to reduce the barriers that departments face in commissioning, conducting evaluations and using the resulting evidence to improve public policies.

Communications and branding

IGEES has certainly made significant progress in establishing a brand for quality economic evaluation within the Irish civil service. Existing stocktaking of papers highlight the quantity of work that is being conducted. However, efforts in this area have to strike a careful balance, between the need to ensure visibility for IGEES while also making sure that the work is being integrated and owned by departments. Now, the production of such documents seems to be driven more by the spending review process and the need for accountability for the resources that have been invested in IGEES.[1]

Issues of branding may also require establishing a logo, as well as possibly some form of social media activity, to socialise the results with the broader public. This may require help from specialised staff, such as communication specialists, data journalists and community managers for rewriting. This might need to be coordinated with government departments' communications units or even the Taoiseach. On that matter, developments of the IGEES website are sought, and a communication strategy is led by the department of Taoiseach. Another type of public could also be the academic community, for example through reaching out to national, European or Northern American research networks (e.g. European Economic Association, National Bureau of Economic Research).

Of course, establishing a communications strategy may require identifying the desirable areas where an increased focus on communication and outreach could be desirable, and achieving a shared understanding across the IGEES policy community within government so that such moves be well understood.

References

Acquah, D., K. Lisek and S. Jacobzone (2019), "The Role of Evidence Informed Policy Making in Delivering on Performance: Social Investment in New Zealand", *OECD Journal on Budgeting*, Vol. 19/1, https://dx.doi.org/10.1787/74fa8447-en. [20]

Axford, N. et al. (2005), "Evaluating Children's Services: Recent Conceptual and Methodological Developments", *British Journal of Social Work*, Vol. 35/1, pp. 73-88, http://dx.doi.org/10.1093/bjsw/bch163. [13]

Brennan, S. et al. (2016), "Design and formative evaluation of the Policy Liaison Initiative: a long-term knowledge translation strategy to encourage and support the use of Cochrane systematic reviews for informing health policy", *Evidence & Policy: A Journal of Research, Debate and Practice*, Vol. 12/1, pp. 25-52, http://dx.doi.org/10.1332/174426415X14291899424526. [22]

Clark, C. (2019), *OMB Moving Ahead to Steer Agencies on Evidence-Based Policymaking - Government Executive*, https://www.govexec.com/management/2019/07/omb-moving-ahead-steer-agencies-evidence-based-policymaking/158381/ (accessed on 16 September 2019). [4]

Department of Finance (2014), "Incorporating Department of Finance Guidelines for Tax expenditure evaluation", http://www.budget.gov.ie/budgets/2015/documents/tax_expenditures_oct14.pdf (accessed on 11 September 2019). [18]

Department of Public Expenditure and Reform (2019), *The Public Spending Code*, https://publicspendingcode.per.gov.ie/ (accessed on 11 September 2019). [15]

Department of the Taoiseach (2009), "RIA Guidelines", https://govacc.per.gov.ie/wp-content/uploads/Revised_RIA_Guidelines_June_2009.pdf (accessed on 11 September 2019). [17]

Epstein, D. and J. Klerman (2012), "When is a Program Ready for Rigorous Impact Evaluation? The Role of a Falsifiable Logic Model", *Evaluation Review*, Vol. 36/5, pp. 375-401, http://dx.doi.org/10.1177/0193841X12474275. [14]

European Monitoring Centre for Drugs and Drug Addiction (2011), "European drug prevention quality standards", http://dx.doi.org/10.2810/48879. [12]

IGEES (2018), "Value for Money Review (VFMR) and Focused Policy Assessments", https://publicspendingcode.per.gov.ie/wp-content/uploads/2018/06/VFMR-and-FPA-Guidelines-Jan2018.pdf (accessed on 11 September 2019). [16]

Japanese Cabinet (2017), "Basic Guidelines for Implementing Policy Evaluation (Revised)", http://www.soumu.go.jp/main_content/000556221.pdf (accessed on 16 September 2019). [5]

OECD (2019), *The Path to Becoming a Data-Driven Public Sector*, OECD Publishing, https://doi.org/10.1787/059814a7-en. [11]

OECD (2018), *Building Capacity for Evidence Informed Policy Making: Towards a Baseline Skill Set*, http://www.oecd.org/gov/building-capacity-for-evidence-informed-policymaking.pdf (accessed on 3 September 2019). [2]

OECD (2016), "The Governance of Inclusive Growth", https://www.oecd-ilibrary.org/docserver/9789264257993-en.pdf?expires=1568647443&id=id&accname=ocid84004878&checksum=8F711F5F9A58B39A458CC239AC893743 (accessed on 16 September 2019). [21]

Office of Management and Budget (2019), *FY2020 President's Budget (Evidence Chapter)*, https://www.whitehouse.gov/wp-content/uploads/2018/06/Gov-. [3]

Office of Management and Budget (2018), *Executive Office of the President Office of Management and Budget Memorandum for Heads of Executive Departments and Agencies*, https://www.whitehouse.gov/sites/whitehouse.gov/files/omb/memoranda/20. [1]

Scottish Government (2019), *Scotland Performs, National Performance Framework, National Outcomes*, https://nationalperformance.gov.scot/ (accessed on 16 September 2019). [19]

The Cabinet Secretariat (2019), *The status-quo about the promotion of statistics reform*, http://www.kantei.go.jp/jp/singi/toukeikaikaku/dai5/siryou1.pdf (accessed on 2 September 2019). [10]

The Committee on Promoting EBPM (2017), *Guidelines on securing and developing human resources for the promotion of EBPM*, https://www.gyoukaku.go.jp/ebpm/img/guideline1.pdf (accessed on 2 September 2019). [9]

The Ministry of Internal Affairs and Communications (2012), "Policy Evaluation Implementation Guidelines", http://www.soumu.go.jp/main_content/000354069.pdf (accessed on 16 September 2019). [6]

The Ministry of Internal Affairs and Communications (2010), "Guidelines for Publication of Information on Policy Evaluation", http://www.soumu.go.jp/main_content/000067741.pdf (accessed on 16 September 2019). [7]

The Statistical Reform Promotion Council (2017), *The final report of the Statistical Reform Promotion Council. (In Japanese)*, http://www.kantei.go.jp/jp/singi/toukeikaikaku/pdf/saishu_honbun.pdf (accessed on 2 September 2019). [8]

What Works Network (2018), *The Rise of Experimental Government: Cross-Government Trial Advice Panel Update Report*, https://assets.publishing.service.gov.uk/government/uploads/system/uploads/attachment_data/file/753468/RiseExperimentalGovernment_Cross-GovTrialAdvicePanelUpdateReport.pdf (accessed on 24 January 2019). [23]

Note

[1] See Hayes and Behan, (2017) a selection of IGEES Output.

Annex A. Papers Published by IGEES since 2016

Title	Department	Year
Social Impact Assessment (SIA): Nursing Home Support Scheme (NHSS)	Department of Public Expenditure and Reform	2019
Social Impact Assessment (SIA): Acute Mental Health Services	Department of Public Expenditure and Reform	2019
Health Workforce: Consultants Pay and Skills Mix 2012-2017	Department of Public Expenditure and Reform	2019
Monitoring Inputs, Outputs and Outcomes in Special Education Needs Provision	Departments of Education and Skills and Public Expenditure and Reform	2019
School Transport Expenditure	Department of Public Expenditure and Reform	2019
Review of Participation in and Costs of Apprenticeships	Department of Public Expenditure and Reform	2019
Review of Carer's Supports	Department of Public Expenditure and Reform	2019
Lone Parent and In-Work Supports for Families and Children	Department of Public Expenditure and Reform	2019
Analysis of Social Housing Acquisitions	Department of Public Expenditure and Reform	2019
Focused Policy Assessment of Capital, Employment, and Training Supports: 2005/2006 – 2018	Department of Business, Enterprise and Innovation	2019
Analysis of Science Foundation Ireland Research Grants	Department of Public Expenditure and Reform	2019
Evaluating the Regional Airports Programme	Department of Transport, Tourism and Sport	2019
Personal Incentives for Electric Vehicle purchase	Department of Public Expenditure and Reform	2019
The Green, Low-Carbon, Agri-Environment Scheme	Department of Public Expenditure and Reform	2019
Beef Data Genomics Programme	Department of Agriculture, Food & the Marine	2019
2016 Heritage Council Review – Assessment of Implementation	Department of Culture, Heritage and the Gaeltacht	2019
Direct Provision: Overview of Current Accommodation Expenditure	Department of Justice and Equality	2019
Trends in Public Expenditure 2019	Department of Public Expenditure and Reform	2019
Valuing Greenhouse Gas Emissions in the Public Spending Code	Department of Public Expenditure and Reform	2019
Rebuilding Ireland – Patterns of Social Housing Construction (2016 – 2018)	Department of Public Expenditure and Reform	2019
Enterprise, Employment and Income Framework: Overview of IGEES Analysis	Department of Public Expenditure and Reform	2019
What is behind aggregate productivity growth in Ireland? A granular approach	Department of Business, Enterprise and Innovation	2019
An Introduction to the Implementation of Green Budgeting in Ireland	Department of Public Expenditure and Reform	2019

Title	Department	Year
Dominant Cities in Small Advanced Economies: Challenges and Policy Responses	Department of Business, Enterprise and Innovation	2019
The Housing Aspirations and Preferences of Renters	Department of Housing, Planning and Local Government	2019
An analysis of Disability Allowance inflows and outflows	Department of Employment Affairs and Social Protection	2019
The Context for NDP Housing Spend: What can the Property Price Register reveal?	Department of Public Expenditure and Reform	2019
Guidance Note #1: The Need for Research	Department of Children and Youth Affairs	2019
Research Briefing: Engagement as a facilitator of school retention and completion: A review of the literature	Department of Children and Youth Affairs	2019
SME Survey 2017	Office of the Revenue Commissioners	2018
Spending Review 2018 - Defence Forces Pensions Expenditure	Cross-departmental	2018
Spending Review 2018 - Agriculture Cash Flow Loan Support Scheme	Department of Agriculture, Food & the Marine	2018
Focused Policy Assessment of Start-Up and Equity Supports	Department of Business, Enterprise and Innovation	2018
Review of the Economic Appraisal Model	Department of Business, Enterprise and Innovation	2018
Statistical Spotlight Series - Young Carers in Ireland	Department of Children and Youth Affairs	2018
Statistical Spotlight Series - Family and Household Structure in Ireland	Department of Children and Youth Affairs	2018
Focused Policy Assessment of the Affordable Childcare Scheme	Department of Children and Youth Affairs	2018
Dominant Cities in Small Advanced Economies	Department of Business, Enterprise and Innovation	2018
Review of the Implementation of the Recommendations of the VFMPR of the Arts Council	Department of Culture, Heritage and the Gaeltacht	2018
Subsidised Ferry Services to the Offshore Islands (DCHG)	Department of Culture, Heritage and the Gaeltacht	2018
An Analysis of Disability Allowance Inflows and Outflows	Department of Employment Affairs and Social Protection	2018
Characteristics and outcomes of jobseekers of African nationality	Department of Employment Affairs and Social Protection	2018
Brexit: Analysis of Import Exposures in an EU Context	Department of Finance	2018
Patterns of Firm Level Productivity in Ireland	Department of Finance	2018
REVIEW OF THE 9% VAT RATE	Department of Finance	2018
An Assessment of Direct Supports for Start-ups and Entrepreneurship (DBEI)	Department of Jobs, Enterprise and Innovation	2018
Review of Criminal Legal Aid (DJE)	Department of Justice and Equality	2018
EU fiscal rules real-time measurement issues of the output gap	Department of Public Expenditure and Reform	2018
Comparative Levels and Efficiency of Public Spending	Department of Public Expenditure and Reform	2018
Brexit: A Sectoral Overview	Department of Public Expenditure and Reform	2018

Title	Department	Year
State Supported Loan Schemes: A Preliminary Analysis	Department of Public Expenditure and Reform	2018
Central Technical Appraisal Parameters	Department of Public Expenditure and Reform	2018
An Analysis of Replacement Rates	Department of Public Expenditure and Reform	2018
SIA Series - National Minimum Wage	Department of Public Expenditure and Reform	2018
Analysis of Live Register Related Expenditure	Department of Public Expenditure and Reform	2018
Public Employment Services – Mapping Activation	Department of Public Expenditure and Reform	2018
SIA Series - Female Labour Market Participation	Department of Public Expenditure and Reform	2018
Pay Expenditure Drivers at Primary and Second Level	Department of Public Expenditure and Reform	2018
Understanding the funding needs of the third level sector	Department of Public Expenditure and Reform	2018
Implementation of recommendations made as part of the VFM and Policy Review undertaken in regard to the Arts Council (DCHG)	Department of Public Expenditure and Reform	2018
Health Budget Oversight and Management	Department of Public Expenditure and Reform	2018
HSE Staff Trend Analysis, 2014-2017	Department of Public Expenditure and Reform	2018
Analysis of Hospital Inputs and Outputs, 2014-2017	Department of Public Expenditure and Reform	2018
Hospital Income - 2013 - 2017	Department of Public Expenditure and Reform	2018
An Analysis of Older People Services Spend and Activity, 2014-2017	Department of Public Expenditure and Reform	2018
Expenditure on General Practice in Ireland	Department of Public Expenditure and Reform	2018
Nursing and Midwifery Expenditure	Department of Public Expenditure and Reform	2018
Efficiency and Digitalisation within the Office of the Revenue Commissioners	Department of Public Expenditure and Reform	2018
Supports for Persons on Low Income	Department of Public Expenditure and Reform	2018
Analysis of Enterprise Supports and the Labour Market	Department of Public Expenditure and Reform	2018
SIA Series - Childcare Supports	Department of Public Expenditure and Reform	2018
Analysis of IDA Ireland Expenditure	Department of Public Expenditure and Reform	2018
Small Advanced Open Economies	Department of Public Expenditure and Reform	2018
Analysis of PSO Expenditure on Public Transport	Department of Public Expenditure and Reform	2018
Trends in General Medical Services (GMS) Scheme	Department of Public Expenditure and Reform	2018
Assessing the Split Between Current and Capital Expenditure on Social Housing Delivery	Department of Public Expenditure and Reform	2018
SIA Series - Social Housing Supports	Department of Public Expenditure and Reform	2018

Title	Department	Year
SIA Series - Assessment of Living Standards during Recovery Period	Department of Public Expenditure and Reform	2018
Review of Overtime Expenditure in An Garda Síochána	Department of Public Expenditure and Reform	2018
Policing Civilianisation in Ireland: Lessons from International Practice	Department of Public Expenditure and Reform	2018
Analysis of OPW Spending on State Rents	Department of Public Expenditure and Reform	2018
Prevention & Early Intervention Series - Aftercare	Department of Public Expenditure and Reform	2018
Prevention & Early Intervention Series - Diabetic	Department of Public Expenditure and Reform	2018
Prevention & Early Intervention Series - Immunisation	Department of Public Expenditure and Reform	2018
Management of Exchequer Pay Bill	Department of Public Expenditure and Reform	2018
Pension Bill Projections for the Public Service: Cashflow Analysis	Department of Public Expenditure and Reform	2018
Spending Review 2018 - Projected Retirements From the Civil Service from 2019 to 2028	Department of Public Expenditure and Reform	2018
Sports Capital Programme (DTTaS)	Department of Transport, Tourism and Sport	2018
Review of Recent Evaluations by DTTaS (DTTaS)	Department of Transport, Tourism and Sport	2018
Evaluation of Budget 2017 Compliance Measures	Office of the Revenue Commissioners	2018
Corporation Tax 2017 Payments and 2016 Returns	Office of the Revenue Commissioners	2018
Income Dynamics and Mobility in Ireland: Evidence from Tax Records Microdata	Office of the Revenue Commissioners	2018
Automation and Occupations: A Comparative Analysis of the Impact of Automation on Occupations in Ireland	Economic Policy Unit	2018
Compositional Analysis of Labour Force and Inactive Working Age Population	Department of Taoiseach	2018
IGEES Work Programme 2017	Cross-departmental	2017
The Irish Government Economic and Evaluation Service Selection of IGEES Output	Cross-departmental	2017
Behavioural Economics Trial - Increasing Attendance at Group Information Sessions	Cross-departmental	2017
The 2017 Evaluation on the Implementation of Ireland's Rural Development Programme 2014 -2020	Department of Agriculture, Food & the Marine	2017
DJEI Review of Capital Expenditure on RD&I expenditure	Department of Business, Enterprise and Innovation	2017
UK EU Exit Trade Exposures of the Irish Economy in a European Context	Department of Finance	2017
COSMO: A new COre Structural MOdel for Ireland	Department of Finance	2017
Income Tax Revenue Elasticities in Ireland: an Analytical Approach, Research Series No.59	Department of Finance	2017
Implications of Behavioural Economics for Tax Policy	Department of Finance	2017
Focused Policy Assessment of Ireland's Bilateral Diplomatic Mission Network in the USA	Department of Foreign Affairs and Trade	2017

Title	Department	Year
Focused Policy Assessment on Met Éireann's International Subscriptions	Department of Housing, Planning, Community and Local Government	2017
Infrastructure Capacity and Demand Analysis	Department of Public Expenditure and Reform	2017
Environment Fund	Department of Public Expenditure and Reform	2017
EU Fiscal Rules and International Expenditure Rules	Department of Public Expenditure and Reform	2017
Climate Change Related Research and Funding in Ireland	Department of Public Expenditure and Reform	2017
Tracking Trends in Public Spending 2017	Department of Public Expenditure and Reform	2017
Analysis of Current Expenditure on Housing Supports	Department of Public Expenditure and Reform	2017
PSO Expenditure on Public Transport	Department of Public Expenditure and Reform	2017
IGEES Learning and Development Framework 2017 to 2019	Department of Public Expenditure and Reform	2017
Targeted Agricultural Modernisation Schemes II	Department of Public Expenditure and Reform	2017
An Assessment of the Rationale, Efficiency and Targeting of Enterprise Supports in Ireland	Department of Public Expenditure and Reform	2017
Review of Social Protection Employment Supports Expenditure	Department of Public Expenditure and Reform	2017
Further Education and Training and Employment Supports Overview Paper	Department of Public Expenditure and Reform	2017
Special Educational Needs Provision	Department of Public Expenditure and Reform	2017
Central Votes Spending Trends and Key Drivers	Department of Public Expenditure and Reform	2017
Increasing Cost of Public Health Sector Pensions Impact on the Exchequer	Department of Public Expenditure and Reform	2017
Future Sustainability of Pharmaceutical Expenditure	Department of Public Expenditure and Reform	2017
Acute Hospital Spending Review	Department of Public Expenditure and Reform	2017
Challenges for Investment in Police Expenditure A Public Expenditure Perspective	Department of Public Expenditure and Reform	2017
The Irish Fiscal Consolidation 2008-2014	Department of Public Expenditure and Reform	2017
An Assessment of the Financial Incentive to Work of Recipients of Illness and Disability Schemes	Department of Social Protection	2017
Working paper: Back To Work Enterprise Allowance – a counterfactual impact evaluation	Department of Social Protection	2017
Jobseeker claims – comparing characteristics and outcomes for casual and full claimants	Department of Social Protection	2017
Transport Trends 2017	Department of Transport, Tourism and Sport	2017
Ireland and the UK – Tax and Customs Links	Office of the Revenue Commissioners	2017
Evaluation of Budget 2016 Compliance Measures	Office of the Revenue Commissioners	2017
Analysis of Low Income Taxpayers and Employer Profitability: Evidence from Tax Records	Office of the Revenue Commissioners	2017

Title	Department	Year
The Oil Market in Ireland – An Update 2017	Office of the Revenue Commissioners	2017
Assessing the level of cross-border fuel tourism	Office of the Revenue Commissioners	2017
SEAI Energy Efficiency Grants	Department of Communications, Climate Action and Environment	2017
GSI Tellus Border Project	Department of Communications, Climate Action and Environment	2016